THE LANGUAGE OF BRITISH INDUSTRY

By the same author
LANGUAGE AT WORK (Heinemann, 1968)
THE LANKY TWANG (Dalesman Books, 1972)
THE YORKSHIRE YAMMER (Dalesman Books, 1973)

THE LANGUAGE OF BRITISH INDUSTRY

Peter Wright

Senior Lecturer in English
Salford University

Macmillan

First published 1974 by
THE MACMILLAN PRESS LTD
London and Basingstoke
Associated companies in New York
Dublin Melbourne Johannesburg and Madras

SBN 333 15359 6

Typeset in Great Britain by
PREFACE LIMITED
Salisbury, Wilts
and printed in Great Britain by
LEWIS REPRINTS LTD
Tonbridge and London

TO MY WIFE

Contents

List of Illustrations   viii
Acknowledgements   ix

Introduction   1

PART A   ORIGINS AND DEVELOPMENT
1   Historical   11
2   New Words   26
3   The Foreign Element   34

PART B   CHARACTERISTICS
4   Changes of Meaning   41
5   Sounds, Grammar and Style   47
6   Bluntness and Friendliness   57
7   Animals and People   61
8   Talking without Speaking   67

PART C   SOCIAL CONTEXT
9   Attitudes to Work and Holidays   75
10   Slang   82
11   Uncouth Language   90

PART D   CAN IT BE UNDERSTOOD?
12   Simplification   101
13   'Help' of the Mass Media   112
14   More Problems   127
15   Unscripted Narrations and Conversations   147
16   General Conclusions   152

PART E   SELECTED INDUSTRIES
17   Household Words   161
18   Coalmining Language   169
19   Steelmaking   181

PART F   FOR THE STUDENT
20   How to Collect Industrial Language   189

     Appendix 1   Etymologies   195
     Appendix 2   Miscellaneous Industries   198
     Select Bibliography   201
     Index   203

List of Illustrations

1   Principal industrial areas   x
2   British coalfields   170
3   Diagram of a blast-furnace   182

Acknowledgements

I am grateful to all informants who have patiently answered some peculiar questions; to my Salford University colleagues, especially Ian Jackson and Alec Shearman, for wise advice and generous help at all stages; to others mentioned in Chapter 18; and to the Athlone Press for allowing me to reproduce the map of British coalfields. Chapter 19 was originally published in *Transactions of the Yorkshire Dialect Society*, 1966.

P.W.

Fig. 1 Principal industrial areas

Introduction

Britain has always had industry. First came farming, then fishing, then other industries; and with them their special words. In this book the term 'industry' is taken in a very wide sense, including for example great modern industries like steel and transport, almost extinct ones like clogging and nail-making, and the all-pervading industries of the mass media and of leisure.

Throughout human history people have worked together — hunters and fishermen for instance — because the group has an evolutionary advantage, and so the language of the occupational group has always been important. This book sets out the anthropological view (what an industrial society and its language are like) and, so far as it legitimately can, the administrative viewpoint (what you can do about them).

The languages of the office, shop-floor, boardroom, bed-sitter, textile mill, pub, dance-hall, football match, building site, coffee bar, etc., are individually fascinating. But they are best understood as part of a general pattern, for many linguistic and social factors at work in one sphere of life appear to a greater or lesser degree in others, and therefore it seemed best to aim at a blend of significant detail against a general background.

It is often said that surveys of industry are too far removed from the dirt and the dust, but it is not intended that such criticism should apply here. This is no exhaustive academic inquiry into the language of one or two industries, badly needed though that may be, but an attempt to foster interest in very striking and important matters. It should be helpful for background work by students of English in technical colleges and polytechnics — indeed anywhere where knowledge of the industrial scene is combined with interest in the English language. In addition it seeks to appeal to the general public, including those who on the contrary may regard much of the subject matter as coming from a strange and remote stratum of society.

1

No detailed linguistic knowledge is assumed. You may not be too concerned, perhaps, about the exact etymology of some glass-blowing expression from inner St. Helens or the precise vowel-quality in a wild-fowling term from Little Muddlecombe-in-the-Marsh; but you may have more than a passing concern about *flats, gazumping, redundancy, output, transistors, tubeless tyres, hamburgers* and so on. Once the general patterns of British industrial language are recognised, you can listen even more eagerly to the experts in your favourite local industry — basket making, baking, brewing or whatever — to see how typical or how odd they really are.

The book has been written as much as possible in non-specialist terms because, if behaviour, conditions or policy are to be influenced, laymen as well as specialists must understand the issues involved. We all need a wide knowledge of different language levels. For instance, the dentist may say to his regular patient, 'You've got a right bad 'un there' but straightway turn to his assistant with 'Upper 3 molar decayed'. The works foreman has to speak not only the same general language as his men — usually no trouble because he has risen from the ranks — but also technical language and the language of trade unionism. Workmen often spend a good deal of their day discussing *form*, i.e. racing form, and their speech often suggests they are leading authorities on it; but at the same time they must grasp the orders and technical terms of their own industry.

Of course, the conclusions drawn in this book are only guidelines, for this is a relatively untapped area of language study. Some suggestions for further analysis are given in Part E, but any study of your own will certainly bring to light further examples and probably other significant trends.

Anything you notice may well be quite important, for communication is a vital social skill. Supervisors and managers need it for shop-floor supervision, higher control, negotiation, committee membership, exchanges of ideas at all levels, and public speaking; personnel staff need it especially for selection interviews and teaching; and workers of all kinds need it for understanding and relaying information, co-operation with their workmates and superiors, and indeed for their own happiness. As work still occupies so much of normal life, we ought to know something about its linguistic character.

WHY INDUSTRIAL LANGUAGE IS SUCH A MIXTURE

Our lives are a constant shuttling about between home and work, club and pub, 'the box' and perhaps the docks, private life and public life. Through encountering different places and people, we have to keep readjusting our language. For instance, you would be a fool to talk in just the same way to your boss, your wife (assuming that is a different person), your vicar at a church gathering, or your workmate who has just fused the lights. Your description of a hammer in buying one from a shop will vary from your description if you bang your thumb with it. Certainly we all have many layers of language.

Firstly there is the influence of Standard English, helped by radio, television, ease of travel and mass education. This, roughly, is the speech of educated South-Easterners (but not Cockney) and gains its status through our capital London, headquarters of British royalty, government, trade, etc., and therefore of speech itself. There is nothing intrinsically snobbish about it, since to be generally understood, especially on more formal occasions, there must be some standard to aim at. Unless the practical capital of Britain shifts, say, to the vast industrial complex of Manchester's Trafford Park, or to Birmingham, or Glasgow, we just have to accept this fact. After all, a captain of industry is likely to create less confusion and a better impression on outsiders by dwelling on his firm's improving prospects in recognised English than by insisting that, say, 'We ain't oddny-dods'.*

WHAT THE MIXTURE CONSISTS OF

A dialect is the speech of a group smaller than the main group who share a common language. English occupational dialects resemble a pyramid, with their height on it determined by socio-economic class and their horizontal position determined by the area where the speaker was born. In other words, we find in them traces of both class and regional dialects. Every conurbation has at least two social dialects (some cities have been proved to contain six). Thus most native businessmen, civil servants and aldermen of any city

*'snails' (Essex term).

will not talk like most of the hotel porters and roadsweepers born and bred there. Although minute differences will be hard to detect, the bigger ones will stand out. Thus, though London bus drivers and taxi drivers may seem to talk alike to you, you should be able to distinguish their language from that of a London teacher or insurance salesman or bank manager with ease. Similarly in Lancashire you may not be able to pick out the Upper Broughton man from the native of Lower Broughton, but effects are cumulative and you might notice a difference in a native of Eccles, still within the Salford boundary, and certainly in the speech of a man from Liverpool or Blackburn.

At the base of the language pyramid, there is the greatest speech difference among farmworkers, miners, inshore fishermen and lower-paid industrial workers; and hardly any at the apex, amongst heads of large firms and industries. The late Lord Melchett's speech resembled that of his typical steelworkers no more than Mr Ezra's does that of his miners.

The most striking features of occupational dialects are their words. Besides general ones similar to those in Standard English, there will be slang, local dialect, vulgar language, abbreviations and much technical jargon, for this is the area of English where dialects and technology cut across each other. Within the same industry, different words for the same idea will be used at different levels or in different circumstances. For instance, where the housewife thinks of *electricity*, the shop-floor term is *juice*, which started in 1920 as electricians' slang and in 1930 reached general slang. Jocularly the term is *gravy*, noticeable when you drop among the *heavy* and the *light gravy men* (those in, respectively, heavy and light electrical engineering); but neither *juice* nor *gravy* is used by research engineers, who would say *current*.

JARGON AND SLANG

Between jargon and slang there is sometimes no clear difference and some dictionaries lump them together. But jargon, the specialised technical language of different occupations and interests, is fundamentally impersonal and serious whilst slang is basically friendly and humorous. To the layman a chemical equation, and to consumers advertisements for products including 'ingredients X, Y and Z', are meaningless jargon.

Each subject has its own trade terms, and to pick on any one as being infested with jargon is wrong or unfair. On occasion, if strangers are present, it is defensive, to prevent their understanding. But amongst themselves industrial workers slip into jargon as they do into a comfortable pair of shoes, because they find it easiest to use.

It is fashionable to poke fun or hurl abuse at jargon as being unintelligible to the outsider, and regrettably this has often been true — it was why Sir Earnest Gowers was asked to write for the Civil Service his excellent handbook *Plain Words* at a time when they certainly needed its more direct language approach. Yet much jargon is a practical necessity. The cricketer needs to refer to *Chinamen, out-swingers, square leg, silly-mid-off* and *leg glances*, whatever the surprised lady spectator may think of some of these terms; the radio engineer to *mike, top* and *fade*. The lawyer, to prevent ambiguity, has to incorporate many an *aforesaid, thereby, hereinafter* or *same*; the engineer mentions a *B.S.308* for a unified thread; both income-tax inspector and taxpayer have to deal each year with an inescapable form known as a *P.60*. Jargon seems destined to say.

Jargon and slang fit different contexts. In the R.A.F. *aircraftsman* is the jargon for a certain rank but *erk* the slang word, *control column* is a technical term but *joy-stick* its slang equivalent. In the R.A.F. during the last war crash landings were *pancakes*, aircraft on fire after being shot up were *flames*, bombs were *eggs* which were *laid*, good was *whizzo* and a successful operation was a *wizard prang*; *kite* is still a plane and *buzzing* another aircraft means flying very fast and close to it in a threatening way. If you consider whether the term is basically serious or flippant, you will soon sense which is slang.

COLLOQUIALISMS AND INFORMAL LANGUAGE

Colloquialisms are expressions used far more in conversation, as their name implies, than in formal written English. In the Standard English-jargon-slang-dialect hierarchy, they may be thought of as occupying the border between orthodox and unorthodox English. *Fed up* is a typical example. The factory office has more formal English than the rest of the works, which normally abounds with slang and colloquial terms. Also, when serious negotiations are going on in the office, especially when representatives have been brought in from different parts of the country, there is more formal language even than usual; whereas outside in the works, in the middle of an *argy-bargy*, you can let yourself fly in light-hearted discussion.

OTHER INGREDIENTS OF INDUSTRIAL LANGUAGE

Slang and technical jargon concern only words, but, because occupational language includes local dialect features, stress, intonation, grammar and pronunciation also enter the picture. When the Workington steelman near the casting bay explains surprisingly *t' yat's theer*, pointing to a small wire-meshed gate beside his electric-arc furnace, *yat* can't be dismissed as Cumbrian dialect from the local farming community and irrelevant to industrial language. If, while his Sheffield counterpart is stopping to eat his mid-morning *snap*, our Workington friend pauses to munch his *bayat*, these words and pronunciations, though from farming dialects, are very relevant to their steelmaking lives. When, for the channel conveying finished steel from the furnace taphole to the ladle, our Cumbrian speaks to officials of the *launder* but in natural conversation with his friends calls it the *lander*, this is significant, not only as another example of steel language but to show how much it varies even in one man's mouth. Occupational speech is highly complicated.

ITS PURPOSE AND ABILITY TO SURVIVE

Although as laymen we may be puzzled by technical matters, somebody has to understand them, which is impossible without appropriate language. A householder, after urgently summoning the plumber, was hardly saving time by telling him, 'The bit what the water comes out of has come out of the bit the water goes through before going into the bit what it should come out of, so now it's coming through the bit it

should be going through to where it should come out of'.*
Exact technical language has it uses.

Whilst it is women who are much readier to abandon
unusual language, chiefly for their children's sake, most
industries remain a man's world. This contributes to the
appearance and survival of the astonishingly vivid industrial
language which we shall now explore. Clearly there will
always be scope for gathering extra information; and, since
this is a continuing piece of research, the author would
greatly welcome comments from readers with anything to
add for a possible future edition.

*Cf. G. L. Brook, *English Dialects.*

Part A Origins and Development

1 Historical

Some people mistakenly believe that industrial language has sprung out of nothing, but industrial words show the same general historical pattern as those in Standard English. The vast majority derive from Old English (i.e. Anglo-Saxon), the English used in this country till about 1150; though significant groups have come in other ways, as shown by the following table, where the biggest groups are indicated by capital letters:

Sources of British Industrial Language

	Celtic
	SCANDINAVIAN
	LATIN
	Greek
OLD ENGLISH	FRENCH
(over 90 per cent)	Dutch, German, Italian, Spanish, N. American
	Miscellaneous languages
	Echoic words; reduplications; folk etymologies
	Doubtful or obscure origin

The complete picture is not so simple because different languages have given us their words during different waves of their linguistic invasions. Yet it is relatively easy, with an etymological dictionary, to trace the histories of individual words. Well over ninety per cent of those in factory-floor and boardroom speech are from Old English. This includes many of the small essential words like *a, that, his, me* and nearly all of the prepositions (*in, to, of,* etc.). Another probable 'home-grown' one is *'em* as in *you've got 'em* which is generally considered lazy speech for *them* (an Old Norse word), but is far more likely to be by loss of *h-* from Anglo-Saxon *hem* ('them'). Also native in origin are many nautical words, like *mast, sail* or *tide* because the Anglo-Saxons were great seafarers.

Words of working are connected mainly with Old English. The farmer(Old English word) milks(OE) his cows(OE), and fodders(OE) his horses(OE) with hay(OE) from the barn(OE). The shepherd(OE) drives(OE) the sheep(OE) to the fields(OE) with his dogs(OE). The inshore fisherman goes out in his boat(OE) with his nets(OE) and lines(OE) holding their snoods(OE) and hooks(OE), and among other things catches sprats(OE), flukes(OE), crabs(OE) and lobsters(OE). Most parts of the body (often referred to during manual operations), like *hand, foot, arm, eye,* or *head,* are from Old English; as are many traders' words like *gold, tin, craft, pin, needle, boots* and *shoes.* Even where people seem to choose a word or pronunciation quite whimsically, like *teeming* for pouring tea or *axe* for ask,* it can go back to Old English. There is no doubt that the nucleus of occupational language is its native element.

The Celtic element is very weak, just as in Standard English. This must be because the Celts, driven out by the Anglo-Saxons to the remote fastnesses of Wales, Cornwall and what is now Cumbria, took with them their Celtic words except for places. This is why a worker even in a partly Celtic-named place like Ilfracombe or Dunster will use very few words of Celtic origin. Those that do occur† in England or even now in the Isle of Man, where the Gaelic-type language of Manx survived till recently, are very rare. A persistent tale is that in remote valleys of Lakeland, Yorkshire and elsewhere the old shepherds still count *yan, tethera, pimp,* etc., using the ancient Celtic sheep-scoring numerals. So many other surprising linguistic features have been found that it would be rash to call it impossible now; but it seems significant that those who claim to know about these numerals always have evidence from a friend who heard them somewhere up a local, usually unnamed valley.

In marked contrast to the small Celtic element, there is however a strong Scandinavian one in occupations in the North and East of England down to East Anglia, i.e. in the Danelaw, where the Vikings raided and settled. Consequently it is no surprise to find there many Scandinavian words like *claggy* (sticky), *addle* (to earn) and *lug* (ear) as in *I'll clout thee on the lug.* But outside that region they are abnormal.

*OE *tāēman*, OE *acsian* respectively.
†E.g. the Lancashire *mullog* (cf. Gaelic *mollag*) 'inflated dogskin buoy'; and Port St Mary *batha-beg* 'dinghy', literally 'boat little'.

You wouldn't expect, say, the Devon farmer or the Hampshire builder to talk about *addling* his wages or having a pain in his *lug-ooal*.

Latinisms in general occupational language are fewer than in Standard English, being too lifeless and vague for it. For particular occupations, however, they have important uses, especially for botanical names and in medicine. If the doctor tells you that you are *nervy* or just prone to *sleepwalking,* you doubt whether he can seriously tackle your illness; it is far more reassuring to be told that your symptoms are of *hypertension* or *somnambulism*, scientific words which sound as if they will readily respond to scientific treatment. Greek also has provided, and still provides, many scientific words — not necessarily spoken by ancient Greeks, but like *television* and *hypotenuse*, made from Greek elements.

One reason for the terminology in biology and botany coming mainly from the classical languages is perhaps that in the fourth century two famous Greeks, Aristotle and Theophrastus, made promising attempts at scientific classification, especially in plants. At first, animals or plants were given only a generic name. However, as more plants or animals which looked similar but in some ways different were discovered, it was found necessary to give them two names, the first for the larger genus and the second for the smaller species, as e.g. *iris pseudacorus* and *iris pumila*, two plants belonging to the same genus *iris*. Biological language has proliferated so much (e.g. through the invention about 1590 of the compound microscope) that its dependence on classical terms has enormously increased. These classical terms are rather difficult to remember and awkward to pronounce, but they provide a good system for accurately describing two partly similar things.

French words appear of course in menus, in general references to work like *machine* and *garage,* in dressmaking and hairdressing (e.g. *costume*, *coiffure*), in architecture (e.g. *terrace*), and in many other specialised cases like the *motty*, a mining term for a tub-label. This last must be from French *mot* (word), as it comes to in the Lancashire criticism of an interfering workmate, 'He's awlus stickin' 'is motty in'. The industrial French element is weaker in Standard English, and more so in the North, where e.g. *folk* (OE) is preferred to *people* (French). Rough and ready occupational language has nothing corresponding to Standard English words from the French like *chic* or *blasé* for conveying slight *nuances* of meaning, or to its French-based words of exceptional politeness. The sewage worker, for example, does not smell a *perfume* or an *aroma*; but, till he gets used to it, he sniffs a native *stench* or *tidy bloomin' stink*.

Dutch is another significant word-group, especially in nautical terms and painting. The reasons are evident: the Dutch were once our greatest rivals at sea as well as nurturing the great masters of oil-painting. Thus *dock, boom, skipper, yacht, sketch, veneer,* etc. Holland has also provided cloth trade terms like *pack, selvedge* and *stripe*; and military ones like *knapsack* and *onslaught*. Nevertheless the Dutch word-element, even in Liverpool, Southampton and our other ports, is relatively small.

Italian is the source of many words in music and the fine arts (e.g. *forte, pianissimo*), besides those connected with food and cookery (e.g. *ravioli, macaroni*); whilst from Spanish come many from war and commerce, like *guerrilla* and *embargo*. German words have reached us in three principal invasions: first, through the science of mineralogy, developed in Germany and bringing words like *zinc* and *nickel*; second, from the meeting of opposing forces in the Great War (e.g. *zeppelin, straf*); and third from the last world war, (e.g. *blitz*). *Swindler* is said to have been introduced by German Jews, though it seems a pity that they alone should be blamed. Since German vocabulary is so closely related to ours, and since that language lends itself very well to the formation of new scientific compounds, it is strange that not till recently did it become a favourite for supplying us with new words.

All major languages of the world have contributed something to the speech of industrial Britain. Arabic is the ultimate source of many scientific words, especially those starting with *al-* like *alkali* and *alcohol*. Our soldiers in India brought back native words like *thug* and *cot*; clothing words like *topi* and *pyjamas*; and the notorious *dum-dum bullets*, named from a place, Dum Dum near Calcutta. Russian is renowned for inventing *sputnik*. American English has given us many words, especially those to do with publicity, like *blurb* and *gimmick*, along with many others such as *radio*, which has replaced *wireless*. As world technologies develop, the supply of new technical words from overseas looks inexhaustible.

Terms have arisen in other ways. There are the back formations, by misunderstanding the function of part of a word. So, for example, we have *baby-sit, burgle, edit, gate-crash, house-keep, tape-record, televise* and *typewrite* as if they had given rise to their corresponding nouns (*baby-sitter*, etc.) and not vice versa. Folk etymology has also been at work, as in *kick the bucket*, slang for 'to die', where, despite suggested theories about standing on a bucket and kicking it away to hang oneself, the real explanation is quite different. Apparently it comes from French *bouquet*, a beam to which the legs of pigs were tied before they were slaughtered.

Still other words come by reduplication, repeating part or all of a word. Parallel to those like *helter-skelter* and *topsy-turvy*, well established in the standard language, come others like the colloquial *ping-pong* for table-tennis, and the jocular *whim-wham* (toy or curious mechanical contrivance), as in 'a whim-wham to wind the sun up with'. Electronics examples are *walkie-talkie, flip-flop* (partly unstable trigger circuit), and *bang-bang* (time-optional control system), which causes noisy jerky plane movements.

The last is also an echoic word, where the sound imitates the sense, and quite a number of words have been formed in this way. A person may *chunner* (grumble), *munch* his food, or *jubber* (talk fast and idiotically). The man in electronics speaks of the *wow* (low-frequency variation, below 10 cycles per second) in the sound from a record-player or tape-recorder, *flutter* for variation above 10 cycles, and *wobbulation* (very low frequency modulation). There is the quick, recurring *clack* of machinery; and, when a painter *wallops* paint on, you can hear the sound as he slaps it about. The spelling *fli-* often represents very light movements, as with *flit* and *flicker*; *slu-* starts a number of horrible words like *slutch* (mud, mire) and *slutherment* (any slimy, viscid matter); and *bl-*, made by inflating the cheeks as in *bleb, blob, blow, blubber*, suggests roundness.

Ask your driver friends to describe the noises from their engines and gearboxes, and you will be surprised at the variety of echoic answers. Their engines *purr* or *tick over* sweetly; *knock, pink* or *tap*; *miss*, or like people *cough* or *splutter*; *clang* when the big end has gone or *blow* through a broken gasket; or *hunt* (i.e. rise and fall, like the sound of a hunting-horn). They complain of their gearboxes *clunging, crunching, grating, grinding, juddering, whining, grawnching* or *scuffuffling*. Older industries have them too. The farm is the home of many strange echoic animal sounds. Here belong, for instance, *moo, quack, grunt*; Derbyshire's *Werp!* (a call to cows in the field); and the Cumberland *dreen* and Devonshire *erge** (with *-ge* as in *rouge*) for the contented sound they make in the cowhouse during milking.

There are always a few words with baffling histories, like *dollop* for a shapeless lump; and words which unexpectedly first appeared in Middle English, such as *pig*, which has replaced Old English *swine* except in special cases like *You dirty swine!*, and *lad* and *lass*. Nevertheless, most factory-floor words have a long pedigree. *Thou girt gawmless gawk!* ('You great stupid fool!') may sound unorthodox but is an interesting historical mixture of two Old English followed by two Scandinavian words.

Occupational language readily forms vivid compounds. If you are past your prime, you are a *has-been*; if lazy, a *never-sweat*; if useless, a *good-for-nowt*. Derivatives include *-less* as in *dateless* or *sapless* to call someone stupid; *-ment* as in *What the hangment!*; and *-ish*. This last suffix (from OE *-isc*) was first used to make national adjectives (*British*), then to mean 'of the nature' (*churlish*), then for resembling visible characterisitics (*shortish, greyish*). Now, however, with years of life and times of day, it also means 'approximately' ('He must be fifty-ish, 'We knock off half-fourish', i.e. finish about 4.30). So far all the examples in this paragraph have been from native elements, but still more effort goes into the concoction and use of foreign additions. In prefixes there is

---

*Phonetically [φy3].

the superabundant use of *super,* and *mini-, midi-* and *maxi-* (e.g. *mini-skirt, midi-length, maxi-collar*). Still more effort, however, goes into using foreign suffixes, e.g.:

-*cade* for spectacles in motion (*aquacade, motorcade*);
-*ex* in trade names (*Sanitex*), believed to be a copy of the *ex-* in *excellent*;
-*eria,* a Spanish suffix now very popular for places where certain goods or services may be obtained (*cafeteria, washteria*) and for other more or less ridiculous Americanised words (*drugteria, shaveteria*);
-*ette* meaning 'small' (*laundrette, majorette*);
-*ique* as in *boutique,* keeping its French spelling, or the monstrous *bootique*;
-*matic* for mechanical appliances (*automatic, hoover-matic*).

Finally there is the diminutive 'friendly' suffix -*ie* or -*y.* It is very popular with women, mostly for articles of dress like *nightie, hanky, nappy, scanties, undies*; but is also used rather flippantly by men. Examples of the masculine use are: *chippy* for joiner; *strappy,* the factory employee who repairs industrial belts; and *clocky,* the man who supervises the clocks where workers *clock in* and *clock out* with their *clock cards.*

Our industries can support words which, though of different origin, are structural parallels and allied in meaning: compare *overseer* (OE) with *supervisor* (Latin), and *overman* or *foreman* (OE) with *deputy* (Latin). Again, one common root can spread to give several spellings and meanings, e.g. *desk, dish* and *disc* (for a record-player). Nevertheless, occupational language, compared with Queen's English, has fewer word-pairs of almost the same meaning. An employee on winning the works sweep will boast of his *luck,* not *fortune*; or admit that someone tackling a mean boss for a pay rise is *brave,* not *courageous.*

Much enthralling history can be in a word. *Posh,* for instance, comes from the initials of *port outward, starboard home,* the way richer passengers used to sail for better scenery off South-West Africa to and from Cape Town. The reason for *starboard* (OE *steorbord*) is that boats were once

steered by oar over the right-hand side of the stern, most
sailors being right-handed. For the other side, OE *bacbord*
became *ladeboard*, probably 'lading or loading side', which
became *larboard*;but, when this was dangerously confused with
starboard in desperate orders during storms, it had to be
changed to *port*. The history alone of occupational words is
fascinating.

Occupational surnames show the importance of work and
its words. After local names like *Ashton* or *Milburn* from
where our ancestors settled, and those like *Jackson* or
McLean meaning 'child of', occupational names form the
next largest group. Almost every village had its smithy, giving
us the 200,000-plus *Smiths* in Britain today, counting
'elegant' variants like *Smythe* and *Smythe-Smythe*. The
wright was till 50 years ago also common in village life. From
the Anglo-Saxon meaning of 'worker' it came to mean
'worker in wood' i.e. joiner or carpenter. Thus we get our
Wrights and surnames compounded from them such as
Plowright and *Wheelwright*. Think too of all the *Carters,
Drivers, Farmers, Fishers, Priests* and *Weavers*, etc., that you
know along with any *Fullers* or *Walkers* (these come not
from hiking but like *Fuller,* from the textile industry),
Butchers, Bakers, Clarks, Millers, Slaters and many more.
Whatever they do or don't do now, all these people can never
escape occupational terminology.

By happy coincidence, some people have been born with
very apt trade-names. A Lancashire *Maltman* is naturally in
the brewing industry. *Fillingham* is a London dentist, and
around Manchester *Mr Orange* is a grocer and a *Macintosh*
sells raincoats. *Counsell, Judge* and *Lawman* have all suitably
chosen law as their profession; whilst *Christian, Faithfull,
Heaven, Love* and *Saint* have all entered the Church, where
they have the best chance to live up to their names; *P.
Shovlin* is a plant-hire contractor; and a Coventry optician
must be delighted with his name of *Hugh Seymour*.

The opposite embarassing result occurs where a surname
seems to put the occupation into a bad light. One city
shelters a butcher *Hackett*, a plumber *Drinkwater*, a funeral
director *Tipping*, a building contractor who is a *Bender*, a
chiropodist *Sillitoe* and dentist *Frankenstein*. Language to

these doubtless hard-working and efficient gentlemen must
be a mixed blessing.

On a more serious note, it is sad — and not just linguistically — that many old trades are dying. The old craftsmen
were men whose word was their bond, doing a job at a fair
price, with a penny or two knocked off 'for luck'. It still
happens, but very rarely.

Returning to language matters, we find that special words
remain from many diminishing, dying or lately extinct
occupations. Many railway terms, like *wezzy* for the two
coaches from the Euston—Liverpool train which continued to
Southport, are dying, often because of electrification.
Another reason is that railways are not closed communities
like steelworks, since railwaymen deal also with the public.
Railwaymen are therefore surprised if their terms are not
generally understood. For instance, *bogies* to them are
obviously coaches. 'Put this in the fourth bogie', one of them
may say to a temporary, and then perhaps, if his helper looks
puzzled, 'Call yerself a university stoodent an' yer don't
know English?'

But railways have seen crazier logic than that. A passenger,
demanding a return ticket and asked his destination, first
replied 'Here'. When the destination had been painfully
elicited and the ticket bought, he burst into uncontrollable
laughter, telling the booking clerk, 'I've diddled you. I'm not
coming back.' And don't forget the ganger who disobeyed
the warning, 'Quick lads, up the banking!' by sprinting along
the line before the oncoming train. Visited in hospital by his
foreman, he explained, 'If I couldn't beat the train on the
level, what chance would I have uphill?'. However, enough
of this. Let's return to sanity with a reminder that the
sophistication of modern railway terms will win — notice that
on the London tubes, the 'degrading' rank of *porter* has been
engulfed in *stationman*.

Clog-making and repairing was till recently a distinct trade.
The *clog-shop* was usually the front room of a terraced
house, and the *clogger* made no attempt at window-dressing
but hung his wares on racks on both sides of the doors. The
shops had a distinctive smell of leather and pitch, and the
clogger wore a leather *brat* (apron) smoothly polished down

the front by rubbing against the last, which he gripped with
his knees. Clog-wearing continued much longer in the North,
e.g. in Warrington, presumably because of the town's 'wet'
industries, brewing, soap and chemicals; but even there the
last clog-shop of any size closed in 1954 and by September
1969, as that month's *Guardian* announced, all had disappeared. Yet clogging expressions are strongly alive, as this
list shows:

1. The *clogger* in football, who ruthlessly hacks down an
   opponent.
2. *Clever clogs.* A term possibly derived from the clog
   dancers — not the folk-art groups, for whom clog-
   dancing seems to be hopping and skipping in the
   manner of morris dancing, but the highly individual,
   quite complicated heel-and-toe tap dancing performed
   by one man, e.g. with the right amount of ale inside
   him outside a pub just after closing time. The term is
   applied derisively by those who don't know something
   to those who do — *Yah, clever clogs!*; or tartly in
   correcting speech or manners — 'All right, we've heard
   enough, clever clogs'.
3. *Empty mi clog.* It is said that in the days before
   indoor W.C.s a lazy man would urinate in his clogs
   rather than leave the house on a very cold night to go
   down th'yard. This may be so, for the phrase was in
   very common use — and most phrases have an origin
   in custom — and is still sometimes heard in the North
   when a group of men are leaving a pub — 'Hold on a
   bit, lads, I'll just empty mi clog'.
4. *To clog.* As well as to re-sole a pair of clogs, it could
   apply to invalids well on the way to recovery — 'Oh,
   he's gerrin' on all right: he'll clog again.' But it could
   also mean 'to threaten violence' — 'I'll clog thee if
   thou'rt not careful.'
5. *Give it some clog* ('Kick hard'). Wigan's great Rugby-
   League full-back, Jim Sullivan, was famous for this.
6. *I'll give mi belly a cloggin'* for 'I'll eat an enormous
   meal.'
7. *He'd sup it out of an old pit clog.* Criticism of any

notorious swiller of ale. Not comparable with the Edwardians who drank champagne from a favourite's slipper.

8. *Tek thi clogs off!* is a command to anyone making too much noise about the house. Billiards and snooker players say something similar when a ball hesitates over a pocket: 'By gow, that ought to tek its clogs off!'

9. *Her face is hard enough to clog* or *She has a face like the back of a clog.* Very unkind comments on an ugly woman.

10. *Get thi clog down!*, a suggestion to a driver that he should accelerate.

Plenty of other occupations supply current terms. From tramcar days comes the driver's saying to his conductor, to hurry the journey along, 'I want you to swing on that bell'. In olden days it was the bell that mattered, not traffic delays as usual now. Of course, the conductor used to pull the strap which rang the bell and now he pushes a button to operate a buzzer, so that in both the old and the modern sense *swing on that bell* sounds wrong.

The *rag-'n'-bone man* appears to have changed from the Steptoe and Son type. They used to be inseparable from back streets, pushing handcarts or sitting on larger carts drawn by ponies or donkeys. They never seemed to collect bones, but presumably at one time they did (on behalf of glue and fertiliser makers?). They would collect rags and junk in general, and in return give housewives abrasive cleaning stones or balloons and celluloid propellers on sticks for the children. They 'cried' their trade, shouting *'agbone!, 'agbone!* as if they had cleft palates, and this chant in the quiet streets before the war could be heard over long distances. Today they tend to be curt young toughs solely interested in scrap metal, but their cries are still heard and their trade is still common. Everyone realises the approach of the *rag-'n'-bone man*, or, as parts of the North call him, the *ragman* or the *tatter*.

The *midden*, as well as being the name for a farm muck-heap, was also applied to ash-pits attached to the W.C.s of terraced houses. Household refuse as well as ash from fires was thrown into them, and they were emptied by corporation refuse squads called *midden-men* who shovelled their contents into the *backs* (narrow alleyways separating one terraced street from another), and then the refuse was shovelled into carts and dumped. This was a particularly revolting job with its own revolting smell: a *midden-man* was as conspicuous as a fishmonger. There was even a song about them, starting:

My father works for the Council;
He empties the middens at night,
And when he comes home in the morning
He's covered all over with —

Chorus: Sweet violets . . .

The *knocker-up* or *chapper-up* has disappeared from cotton towns. He performed a very useful service before alarm clocks were introduced. He used to walk from house to house about 5 o'clock on workday mornings, rapping with his long cane at the bedroom windows of his clientele until they wakened and shouted down to him. For his services he charged a few pence a week (six days then) to anyone who made use of him. Miners also employed a *knocker-up*, but nowadays in an emergency they are called out by the mine's *lurry-driver*.

Uncles (pawnbrokers) with their *pop-shops* began to disappear after the 1939—45 War, but before that there was one, under the sign of three brass balls, in every working-class district. Such shops often had separate entrances for those borrowing or redeeming. For many families the *pop-shop* was a necessity, and for such it was no music-hall joke to *pop* the Sunday best into pawn every Monday morning and take them out of it every Saturday night.

Before the days of bread-making 'factories', there were many small bakers who delivered most of their bread daily from house to house. Most used horse-drawn vans but some pulled man-drawn wheeled boxes. Some of these bakers managed also to corner their local muffin and crumpet market. In another old industry, *bread* was quite a different food. In many old Yorkshire farmhouses can be seen, hanging from the ceiling, racks which are still called *breead*(bread)-*flakes*. *Bread* here means 'oatcake', and it was on these racks that oatcakes were hung.

Before the organisation of big dairy combines, most local milkmen were farmers who had cattle. Their cry would be "Ilk! 'Ilk! Penny a quart!' Up to the late 1920s milk was normally bought from a horse-drawn cart, in which were churns, gill and pint measures, and cans. The *gill* was a half pint. Before household *fridges* were thought of, it was never practical to buy more than one day's supply of milk. Also before the *Fridge Age* fresh fish shops were few because the fish trade was a precarious one for retailers. An out-of-town and very welcome tradesman, therefore, was the occasional fisherman who might drive inland in a horse-drawn cart selling, in South Lancashire for example, mostly flat-fish like dabs and plaice-flukes, and cockles and mussels — the last two by the measure, a gill or pint. They too would cry their wares. If you happened to live in Newcastle, you would probably appreciate the calls of Newbiggin fishwives coming into the city and shouting *Caller hah'n!* ('Fresh herring!').

Various other artisans had their street-cries. Gypsies had 'Pegs to sell!' Other vendors called, 'Pots, kettles and pans to mend!'; or 'Scouring stone, yoller or white, penny a lump!'; or 'Old 'ats I buy; jam-jars, stone jars or any old iron'. Round some areas in winter would come a man carrying a cylindrical can, its fretted lower part filled with red-hot coke, and shouting 'Peas, peas, all 'ot!'

In Liverpool, St John's Market in *Great Charlotty Street* has been pulled down and the last *shawlie* has plied her trade, though the word remains in more general use there for any old lady, with or without a shawl. In all our cities, *barrer-boys* are lasting longer than expected, with their particular cries and techniques. Next time you pass their sloping *barrers*, notice how the weights are always placed on the lower scale, and how they often slap down on it the last item of fruit in any quantity they are selling. Surely local inspectors of weights and measures must for years have been turning a blind eye to these practices, to the annoyance of local rate-paying shopkeepers.

But the real strugglers seem fewer. Ignoring the gypsies (or *romanies* or *didicoys* as they have been called), in the non-affluent society before the 1939—45 War the unemployable were condemned to an existence more precarious than a wild animal's. Cripples, the chronic sick, the blind, the deaf, the dumb and the mentally sub-normal — any not physically capable of labouring or lacking the intelligence to learn a trade — were condemned to scratch a living as best they could. From these people came the street-corner sellers of matches, *boot-whangs* (bootlaces) and shoddy novelties; the pedlars who went from home to home carrying their stock in small suitcases; the sellers of bundles of *kindling* (chopped firewood), which they carried in old prams and home-made trucks. Socially it is good that some of these trades have gone, even with their picturesque cries and words.

Many terms have moved across industries, rail terms providing outstanding examples. The railwaymen of the nineteenth century did not spring from nowhere, without background and traditions. Some appear to have come from the coaching world, introducing its vocabulary. From stagecoach days come *coach* itself, the *quarter-lights* for the corner windows in the older-type railway compartment, the *undercarriage*, the *booking office*, and the shout *Right away!*

In explaining that you feel *under the weather*, have *steered clear* of bronchitis but have *landed up* with a touch of flu, you are of course using nautical language. The bus expression *getting a head of steam on* comes from the steamships; and another transport term, *the bus* (or *car*) *won't pull*, is from the days of the horse and cart.

Some words have moved from farming to mining. Durham miners relish their *bait* and Nottinghamshire miners their *snap* from their *snap-bag*, originally farmers' terms from the practice of feeding horses out of nosebags in the fields. Farming has also given mining *strick*,* a measure of rubbish put into a *tram*, from an Old English word meaning measure of corn; and *goaf*† for the large mine-cavity from which coal has been extracted. It also apparently gives *pens* from cattle

---

*OE *stricel*, cf *EDD*, *strike*, sb.[1]
†Cf. *EDD*, *goaf*, sb.[1], 2.

markets to enormous containers for scrap in the steel industry. Out of the building industry comes *talking bay winder* for speaking affectedly, a biting criticism even in these days when houses have more modern improvements.

The steel industry allows others to use some of its words. Ebbw Vale workmen whose houses had a sink call it a *bosh*, reserving *sink* for the drain it emptied into. *Bosh* must have come from the town's iron and steel industry, where it means the lower part of a furnace. Significantly *bosh* was never used by Forest of Dean miners in Gloucestershire, a farming county. We also hear of *teeming** tea into cup and of the rain *teeming* down, comparable with *teeming* for pouring molten metal; and from the old puddling furnace, of someone being *puddled*, with his mind, so to speak, whirled around until he goes silly. A word that our steel industry has exported is French *cubillot* from British *cupola* for the casting furnace.

In more modern occupations and interests, the railway term *shunt* has taken a new lease of life for the commuter or motor-rally driver who bumps into another vehicle, whilst *prang* for crashing a car is from Air Force slang. *Output*, from the steel industry, appears in *computer output*, etc. *Hardware* also is leaving the ironmongers for the computer industry, where it stands for the computer itself as opposed to the paperwork programmed into it, and to the peculiar *liveware*, the computer operators. Thus, in word movements across industries, much language history goes on.

*From OE *tāēman.*

2 New Words

Of the many interesting ways in which new words appear, the commonest is through technical language. Technical words for new ideas are constantly appearing, and many struggle to enter the standard language. Of those which do, many, like *electricity, symptom* and *thermometer*, have become part and parcel of the layman's speech. Just as the Greek words *fancy, idea, pathos* and *sympathy* lost their original psychological meanings to acquire in English more general ones, so the man-in-the-street will now bandy about words like *extravert* or *ego* with no idea of their earlier significance.

Other words (e.g. *sputnik*) come in directly from abroad. This is common during wars, when opposing forces confront each other, attacking and counterattacking with men, weapons and words. From the Great War came, e.g. *zeppelin, no-man's-land* and *zero hour*. From the last there was a host of others, including *black market, call-up, cease-fire, concentration camp, convoy, doodlebug, evacuation, fire-watcher, paratroops, quisling, ration-book* and *war bride*; and recent threats of conflicts have produced, e.g., *cold war* and *war of nerves*.

A third source of new words on the factory floor is slang. Much of this grows and dies very quickly, but some is powerful and resilient enough to stay and become widely acceptable. Of this type are words like *bully, mob, bamboozle, jazz, jeep, jitters* and *bulldoze*.

A fourth but rarer way is for a term to spread from local dialect to industrial speech, and then sometimes more widely still to the standard language. A good example is *slurry* (thin watery mud), which became notorious throughout Britain because of the 1966 Aberfan disaster (even as answer to the ghoulish riddle, 'What's black and shiny and goes to school?'), whilst *billy*, another South Wales term for it, stays comparatively unkown. *Telegawping* for watching television intently belongs partly to this class, since it comes from the Greek element *tele-* meaning 'far', plus the general dialect word *gawp* for staring with wide-open mouth.

Since industrial language — and the standard language — gain fewer words from dialect than from the first three processes mentioned above, it is remarkable to find words like the following apparently restricted in earlier days to dialect. A search through the 1904 *English Dialect Dictionary* will show, e.g., that *taxman* was then thought only a Scottish word (this takes some believing!), an *overall* and *hard-core* appeared only as Lancashire terms, and *puff* ('verbiage', as in *advertisers' puff*) and the trawling term *otter-boards* were apparently limited to Yorkshire. Similarly *locker* was then, it would seem, restricted to Westmorland, Yorkshire and Derbyshire; *wanky* (weak and feeble) to Cumberland and East Anglia; and *squelch* to Scotland, Ireland, Northumberland and Berkshire. If the dialect correspondents of that time were able to report the true situation, it must have greatly changed since, for all these expressions are now used far more widely.

A consideration of the same dictionary shows how new much industrial language is. Although the chief preoccupation of that work is of course with dialect, many industrial terms are also recorded; but they include terms from a number of industries, or parts of industries, which are now obsolescent or extinct — the vocabularies of, e.g., black-smiths, hedgers, millers, peat cutters, scythers, thatchers, threshers, wheelwrights and winnowers. Do you know, for example, what all of these things are? — *bullernecking*, a *flail, grass-nibs*, a *groom.* * You will be most knowledgeable if you do.

Occasionally an established word drops out to be replaced by a new one. Thus it is more modern to refer to *polio* than infantile paralysis, *spastics* instead of sufferers from cerebral palsy, and *thrombosis* instead of a stroke or blood-clot. On the other hand, some experts, thoughtlessly or in a desire to air their knowledge, talk to the layman in terms which, though more exact, are incomprehensible to him; using e.g. *carcinoma* for cancer, or *oedema* for a type of ankle swelling. If you want to, the best way to deflate them is to say frankly

---

*Respectively turning peat sods on to their opposite ends; a stick with a leather thong attached, for threshing; the pair of handles jutting out from the long shaft of a scythe; and an iron rod for combing down the thatch.

that you don't understand and ask them to explain in ordinary language.

Of course, many ideas which were once new, like *radiogram* or *helicopter*, are now no more. Moreover, the process of choosing one word from several is sometimes not yet finished. Thus for rubber-soled canvas shoes we have *pumps, plimsolls, gym-shoes* and *squeakers*, three of which should eventually go to leave just one expression. On official notices *lay-by* is prominent, though many motorists and *The Penguin English Dictionary* prefer to call it a *pull-in*.

It is rather an arbitrary matter which new words at any moment become acceptable. For example, among words that since 1961 have come into use or need redefining, all causing problems for the dictionary makers, are *antinatalist* (advocate of population control), *convertibility, ecocide* (wilful destruction of natural environment), *Eurodollar,* and *stagflation* (inflation by severe price-wage inflation at a time of stagnant consumer demand). Other new ones now being met are *gazumpers, containerisation* and *transportation*. The snag is that large dictionaries take so long to compile that they are somewhat out of date before they are completed. A more useful guide for current words and meanings is a smaller, carefully written modern one like *The Penguin English Dictionary*. But an even better way, if you are thinking of Standard English, is to observe the writings and remarks of living educated people; or if you are considering technical language, as we are, to notice the terms now being used not only by distinguished technologists but also on the shop floor. In this way you should become more up to date than the writer of the best technical dictionary.

Some cantankerous people object to any new word because they hate any change. They object to comprehensive schools, decimalisation, the Common Market, shorter working weeks, longer holidays — anything new. Everything, they believe, was better in 'the good old days'. Despite such resistance, new words keep appearing, and nowhere more strikingly than with names for recent sciences. How many of these can you identify, for many people have to know all about them? — aerostatics, audiology, biometrics, cybernetics, ecology, gynaecology, geriatrics, industrial archaeology (that sounds an awkward one!), occupational therapy, phonemics, reprography, tribology.

Here are some words lately accepted, first into technical and then into general written English. See how far you can extend each set in, say, five minutes, checking afterwards in a recent dictionary (though, as just explained, this cannot give quite the last word):

Trade terms — cellophane, cornflakes, nylon, penicillin, polythene, sellotape . . .

Industrial war and peace — closed shop, assembly line, cost of living, dollar gap, go-slow, one-off job, work-to-rule, wage freeze . . .

Air transport — airlift, jumbo jet, test pilot, sound barrier . . .

Clothes and fashion — bikinis, bras, jeans, stiletto heels, T-shirts, windcheaters . . .

Domestic, — baby-sitter, carry-cot, pressure cooker, shopper . . .

City words — commuter, conurbation, rush-hour, smog, parking meter, rat-race . . .

Mind you, in pockets there is great resistance to new technical terms. People argue vehemently that old aircraft names like Spitfire, Hurricane and Mosquito were more proper than, e.g., Boeing 707, half of which is a mere number; that an address like 4 Cherry Tree Avenue is more genuine than a postcode like GF3 8UH; that Spaghetti Junction is a better name than what the motorway planners tried to call it; that a private telephone number like Stockport 3086 loses its identity when it becomes 480–3086. For this type of unfeeling treatment some obstinate people try to get their own back. One customer, after vainly attempting to describe the ice-cream he wanted, was told curtly, 'You mean a 99, mate'; so next week he asked for '495'. 'Whatever's that?', asked the baffled salesman. Quick came the answer — 'Five 99s'.

The faster-growing the industry, the more new terms it needs, and nowhere is this more evident than in electronics. Since 1940 this field has widened so much that the student and even the scientist find it hard to keep up with new developments. These have been spectacular and have touched almost every branch of human activity. The new techniques have revolutionised the arts and radio and telecommunications, put important tools into the hands of the research scientist, the applied mathematician and the surgeon, and have helped numerous branches of industry. Consequently many engineers and technicians, originally trained in a different line, now have to apply electronic techniques to their own workday activities, or to install, adjust and maintain electrical equipment.

Thus a growing number of scientists and technicians have to become acquainted with new electrical terms — which is harder than it sounds, for often the spate of new books assumes that the reader, even the specialist, is far more familiar with recent terminology than he actually is. The result is a mass of people, fairly knowledgeable about one branch, trying to familiarise themselves with others and the techniques used in them, which naturally involves learning a new vocabulary.

Over great stretches of industry there is a tendency to create new non-dictionary verbs, like *'e's bin rostered* (put on the roster), *that phone-box has been vandalised* (damaged by vandals), or *I gassed up* (filled my car's petrol tank).

The last is also a reminder of the many Americanisms creeping into British English. It happens most in television and advertising. *Blurb* and *gimmick* are now in our latest dictionaries, and the adjective *gimmicky* may soon enter. Wireless, a word covering all types of radio-communication and still used by the elderly, has been largely replaced by the American term *radio*. Recent electronics magazines show that *antenna* is beginning to oust *aerial*, and *electron tube* starting to supersede *valve*, even though the American expressions are longer; whilst *program*, despite its American spelling, is now accepted for the scheme fed into a computer. Words do flow both ways across the Atlantic, but under the influence of Uncle Sam we import far more than we export.

We haven't, however, accepted American terms *en bloc* and without question. Our cars are not *automobiles*; and their engines are under bonnets, not *hoods* as in the U.S.A., because *hood* with us is what in the States is called the *top*.

Our vehicles have silencers, not the American *mufflers*, which could be confused with our regional word for 'scarves'. This happened to an English lecturer in the States in very hot weather: he was startled by a patrolman who, hearing his car's noisy exhaust, asked 'Where's your muffler?'. Our flats have not yet become *apartments*, nor have our lifts turned into *elevators*, and we post, not *mail*, letters. But the influx of Americanisms is far from finished.

Wherever they satisfy a need, new technical words will appear. Changes in knowledge, inventions and culture often cause them. Thus the gramophone has been superseded by the new machines *record-player* and *tape-recorder*. But, once invented, new words don't stay still. Some widen in meaning, and of these an interesting set, which has moved on into Standard English, are those formed by co-opting a particular product name to become the general term for all such objects. Thus a *hoover* now stands for most vacuum cleaners, not just for the appliances of the original firm; *biro* for any ball-point pen; and *elastoplast* for all sticking plaster. Other new terms narrow in meaning or in sections of industry where they are used. *Trunking* used to mean only night driving, but now, because of improved roads and speeds enabling travel to and from a far unloading point in one day, it includes *day-trunking*. *Clocking on and off* under the watchful eyes of the *clocker* or *clocky* is the practice in many a works, but bus drivers and conductors have instead to *sign on* because they are dealing with the public. They may have to make a personal appearance before the traffic inspector to show that they are not drunk or otherwise unfit. Once, around Manchester for example, they would not be signed on if they were without a hat, clean shoes or tie; but, if their appearance was satisfactory, for that alone they would receive the equivalent of 17½p. Conditions may have eased, but they still need to *sign on*.

Considering that some industries are so old, it is surprising how many hitherto unrecorded words they possess. Yet they must have been on workpeople's lips for many years. All their absence from well-known dictionaries* means is that

*E.g. the big *Oxford English Dictionary* (1884–1928) and Joseph Wright's monumental *English Dialect Dictionary* (1904).

contributors to those works had not met them; for even the
dictionary-makers and their untiring helpers could not hope
to unearth the origins, home areas, pronunciations and
meanings of every word then alive in Britain. Such apparent
discoveries include, in coal mining for example; *yawks* for
straps or string tied round trouser ankles; *spake* (Glamorgan),
man-rider (Leigh) and *paddy* or *paddy-rider* (Cheshire, West
Yorkshire) for the set of carriages for conveying miners;
peggy and *noper* for the tool commonly called a pick;
connies for a gold-coloured vein in coal; the Scottish *glenny
lamp* for detecting gas and *glenny-blenk* (blindness); and
gobbin for a rock fissure from which gas escapes.

Intelligent guesses, however, might link some of these
terms with known words — *yawks* with a dialect word
meaning 'to grip', *glenny-blenk* with a Shetland and Orkneys
term for peeping through half-shut eyes, and *gobbin* with the
slang word for mouth as in 'Shut thi gob!'

Sometimes an expected Standard English and widely
known word does not appear because workers use another
word for it. Where there are no *boys* or *girls*, there are *lads*
and *lasses* (or in parts of Lancashire *wenches* or in the
South-West *maids*). A worker may talk about his *lad* or *lass*
instead of his son or daughter, and will certainly say *our
Jack's wife* instead of *my daughter-in-law*. Similarly, a
workman may seem to have no *yes* or *no* or *perhaps*: he can't
talk without using equivalents, normally *aye, nay* and *'appen*.
For 'yes', two unexpected variants are at large. The South
-West and South-West Midlands have *ah,* which first sounds to
a stranger like an uncalled-for exclamation; and Lancashire
has *yigh*, but only to contradict — e.g. 'You didn't!' 'Yigh, I
did.' *Evening*, though it appears on notice boards, is not a
real word in factory speech; and this tallies with the custom
in many rural parts of England, where the evening greeting is
Good Neet!

Many words well recorded for industrial language about
seventy years ago* seem to have died out. Such are *stob* and
ruin for the all-purpose area where miners brewed up,
urinated, hid from the *gaffer*, etc. This is now usually the

---

*In the 1904 *English Dialect Dictionary*, whose author does not usually
distinguish between dialect and occupational language.

gob, because it resembles a big mouth. Other apparently extinct mining examples are *clour* for a roof depression, *vug* for a rock cavity, *gird* and *tack* for a small prop of wood or coal, *wamp* for very fine sand thrown down mines to prevent explosions, *colley* for coal-dust, and *stinker*, an appropriate name for coal which when burnt emits a disagreeable smell. There is no absolute proof that such words are dead, but they are very difficult or impossible to find now (except in books, which is not the same thing), and what has happened in mining is typical of a dead element in most industries.

More surprising are the absences of certain other words and ideas. A few of these must be put down to ignorance. There was, for instance, the lorry driver observed under a bridge, where the headroom was just an inch or so too low, frantically trying to pull down stonework at the top of the arch. 'Why don't you let your tyres down a bit?', asked a helpful passer-by. 'Nay', answered the stupid driver, 'it's the roof of my lorry that won't go under, not the wheels.' If a fellow like that has no word for some well-known object, ten to one he never uses it or thinks about it.

Nevertheless, most absences of words can easily be explained. In inshore fishing, the reason for long stretches of the English and Welsh coastlines having no words for the coble is just that those places never had such boats; where local words for the parts of a crab- or lobster-pot are unknown, this is simply because the coast there is too shallow and sandy for such fishing. On the comic plane, compare the would-be tenant who said, 'There's a nasty smell in this flat. Are you quite sure the drains are clear?', and the landlord's reply, 'It can't be the drains. We have none'. If the things aren't there, you can't rightly demand a word for them.

Snobbery dictates why *streets* are disappearing, although there is a growing surfeit of *avenues, closes, groves, lanes,* etc. The reason for an inshore fisherman avoiding standard nautical expressions, like *north-by-east, south-by-west*, is that he considers them book terms, preferring vaguer ones like *Keep her* (the ship) *off a point, t'wind's comin' out o' t' northern* ('from somewhere near south). Apart from a few exceptions like those above, normally any precise technical idea demands a special word to explain it exactly, which is why industrial language seems bound to keep growing.

3 The Foreign Element

A seemingly foreign element in English industrial language is caused by an attempt to 'pass the buck' and blame anything bad on those foolish enough to be born in another country or a 'backward' part of Britain. In our general language, a window that is not a real window because it can be opened and walked through is a *French window*; and for similar reasons we have *German measles, French leave* and *French letter, Dutch treat, Scotch egg, to talk Irish* (nonsense), and *to Welsh*, as if only the Welsh are capable of running away from their debts.

Industry has similar expressions. A barn without sides and therefore only masquerading as one is a *Dutch barn*; and an auction which is false because the bidding goes down instead of up is a *Dutch auction*. An *Irish daisy* is a dandelion, and an *Irishman's rise* is actually a fall in wages. One of the oddest linguistic creations is the *Scotch French loaf*, so called because it is baked in what is termed a *French pan* (rectangular and about 3 ft long) and traditionally eaten in Scotland. After that monstrosity it seems almost normal to call margarine *Dutch* (or *French*) *butter*; and, again criticising the eccentricities of the Irish, to say *Put it on Paddy's shelf* (the floor). Somewhat truer but still exaggerated is *Bhowani Junction* for Southall Station, which gained its new name through being used by so many Indians and Pakistanis, and because British railwaymen can't tell which is which.

British places exciting memories of far-flung parts of the world have unusual origins. Various hamlets labelled *Egypt* dotted around our counties are apparently called from gypsies who dwelt there; whilst *New York*, a collection of dwellings at a cross roads, that a motorist meets suddenly in Lincolnshire, was allegedly named by a hopeful builder who wanted it to expand as fast as the American capital. Not so different is the term, now rapidly gaining ground, e.g. among decorators, *working foreign* or *doing a foreigner*. It has nothing to do with commuting, say, as a few lucky executives now do to a Common Market country; but means working privately, unknown to the Inland Revenue, to supplement one's regular wage.

Local pride and laughter at customs elsewhere result in other curious descriptions, like the *Irish screwdriver* or *American screwdriver* for the hammer. Manchester electricians call it a *Birmingham screwdriver*, believing that only *Brummagers* could be so daft as to work on the principle, 'If you can't fit it, hit it': whilst *Brummagers* retaliate by calling it the *Manchester screwdriver*. Similarly. Derbyshire folk insist that goitre, often called *Derbyshire neck*, is *Manchester neck*. Another linguistic let-down is the Lancashire term *Irish boiled ham* for what proves to be a cheese barm-cake from the works canteen. References, therefore, to other areas are usually disparaging. Conversely, where the thing described is too good to be laughed at, it may lose its county element. This happens with those slightly sweetened, crisp buns called in Standard English *Devon splits*, which in Cornwall are just *splits*, with no jocular reference to the neighbouring county, and in Devon itself *cut-runs* (cut-rounds).

As for the genuine foreign element in English, the strangest situation at the moment concerns Welsh. In the Welsh-speaking districts of North and Central Wales remarkable mixtures crop up. An English visitor has only to listen to any Welsh conversation to be struck by the sudden appearances of English trade names like *cornflakes* and expressions like *O.K.* for which apparently there are no suitable Welsh equivalents. Nor are these the only types of mixture. For the cardinal compass points, the North Wales fisherman uses the Welsh *gogledd, de, dwyrain* and *gorllewin* (N.,S.,E.,W.), but for all the intermediate points chooses English. For the seats of a dinghy he uses neither the English *seat* nor the Welsh *sedd* but the corruption *sayt*; whilst for a codling, using an English noun with a Welsh adjective but in Welsh word-order, he says *cod bach*.

In South Wales and Monmouthshire there are curious relics of Welsh. Ignoring the strangeness of English-named firms operating in counties bristling with awkward Welsh signpost -spellings, there are still the oddities of what spoken Welsh is left, a good case being that of Ebbw Vale. In this area, once quite agricultural but by 1911 completely industrialised, up to 1780 the English language was unkown. From 1860, however, the Welsh language there began markedly to decline through heavy immigration from Ireland and from English-speaking districts all round the Severn. Today Welsh, which in 1930 was still spoken by some of the elderly inhabitants, has effectively disappeared, and to trace it one might well have to go to the Neath valley some twenty miles west. This situation has brought about translations like the colliery name *Coalbrook* for *Nantyglo* ('stream of coal'), translated from the once-vigorous Welsh; and corrupt Welsh, as in the Heol-y-Mwyn Hotel in Ebbw Vale, which lost its Welsh pronunciation, roughly *Hale-a-Moin*, to become *'Ole-i-Moin*. This decay of Welsh is naturally linked with the needs of Welshmen seeking jobs in non-Welsh-speaking areas to be fluent in English. Yet they are reluctant to be completely Anglicised. One of them working near Coppull in Lancashire was heard to remind his *butty*, 'Thee bisn't a bloody Lanky, thee bist a bloody Welshman'.

A serious charge often made is that many foreign-born doctors practising in this country, especially Indians, cannot understand our language and therefore cannot diagnose and prescribe accurately. But the General Medical Council has been quoted in the national press as claiming that it would be 'unnecessary, undesirable and impracticable' to test overseas doctors' grasp of English before they are allowed to practise here. Also, they can't be adequately warned against all the weird complaints that our working population chooses to have. Commonly in English factories blisters are *blebs*; fists are *neefs* or *naves*; and splinters can be *spelks, spiles, spoals* or *stobs*. Geordie workers' hands tend to get *hacked* or *keened* instead of chapped; a whitlow may be a *bustion (Lancashire) or plook* (Yorkshire), whilst there are *twilly-toed* people and those with the opposite disfiguration who are *sprottle-footed*. Of course, linguistic difficulties are not all on one side. Overseas doctors' own stress and intonation no doubt seem so odd to their patients that language barriers are unconsciously magnified; but without overseas doctors our health service would collapse. Many are highly skilled, all are hard-working, and much more should be done where necessary to assist their English.

The linguistic problems from immigration have been increasing. In all occupations, spoken English tends inevitably to become distorted in the mouths of immigrants with names like *Ilczyscyn* and *Kovacevik*, though they have to use our language. For one thing, if foreigners speak in their own tongue and the British workman is *stood there like piffy* (standing by helplessly), he will pull their legs; for another, some of them have never worked before in British industry and so tend to accept local terms, even if they can speak only broken English; but, thirdly, many are naturalised and now talk English even amongst themselves. Foreign names will often be shortened and if possible Anglicised. *Nic* — will become *Nick, Ivanovski* will become Ivan, *etc.* Jan Ball, *a Pole working at Leigh, who used to be nicknamed 'am bone*, naturalised himself to *John Bold* and now is known usually just as *John*. It is a typical instance.

The extent to which the overseas language barrier is sometimes disappearing is shown by an official complaint lodged recently by a Pole at Leigh Miners' Club against weekend overcrowding of their facilities. He argued, 'Our own people can't get in for all these bloody foreigners from Manchester'. The same kind of thing is happening in other areas. A Bradford teacher of an immigrant class went to considerable trouble to learn a little Urdu, but when he tried it on his class was met vacantly by *Yerwhat?* and the grudging acknowledgement that some of them were learning a bit of it themselves. A foreigner at a Dewsbury blanket mill greeted an English friend with, 'Goot mornink, Roger! How arta gooin' on?' Unlike the previous incidents the next cannot be vouched for, but the story is circulating strongly in the library world that a reader asking for a book on Urdu was directed to the section on hairdressing.

In fact, a weight of evidence shows that British industrial language has hardly been dented by the overseas element. The fear may be that coloured people entering our country may eventually colour our language, but isolated words like *char* and *thug*, brought long ago by the British from India, are negligible evidence. Something more will have to affect English before we admit any significant overseas influence. However hard it is to explain, most of us immediately recognise the peculiar stress and intonation of a West Indian or Pakistani speaking English. Only if a large proportion of British workers starts to stress and intone words like that, or brings in foreign vocabulary wholesale, or (like Arab, African and Malayan speakers of English) ignores many a *the*, shall we be able to say that the British element is starting to submerge. The same applies to any influence from the European Economic Community, for in their different ways French and Germans, for example, however well they know written English, will always find it difficult, if not impossible, to achieve a truly British stress and intonation. The same applies even to speakers with a Welsh background. Thus the present situation is clear: the overseas element in English factories and occupations, so far from influencing our industrial language, is being swamped by it.

Part B Characteristics

4 Changes of Meaning

At the outset, in dealing with changes of word meaning (or semantics), we must realise we are on very tricky ground, as almost every dictionary word has by now acquired more than one meaning, and a few, like the indispensable *get*, sixty or more. For instance, many a girl has maintained that she will never be dictated to and then become a shorthand typist, and unemployed restaurant managers have been told at labour exchanges to wait. In seriously investigating the antics of semantics, five main processes have to be borne in mind:

1. *Internationalisation*, taking a word from another language, and often in doing so rather changing its meaning. Shown in Chapter 1.
2. *Elevation*, by which unstandard language (technical, colloquial, slang or dialect) becomes standard. See Chapter 2.
3. *Degradation*, the opposite of the last and rarer. Here a word is relegated from Standard English to the 'lower divisions' of dialect. An example is *lug* for ear, which occurs in the well-known Middle English poem *Sir Gawayne* but is now very dialectal. Other examples are: *while* for until (e.g. *Wait while seven*), found in Shakespeare but now branded as 'iggerant' Northern English; *quick* or its alternative regional pronunciation *wick* for alive, as in *quick/wick wi' mawks* (alive with maggots); *meat* for food, as in *I'm off mi meat*; and the common *I'll learn you*, although this last, when used ironically, has the unstandard meaning of 'I'll teach you never to do that again', not 'I'll formally instruct you'.
4. *Narrowing*, where a general word becomes particularised. Thus the general word *warden*, from the same root and with the same meaning as *guardian*, came to mean the warden of a students' hall of residence, a prison warden (who is, despite students' claims, very different), in the last war an air-raid warden, and now,

seemingly ready to flick open his or her notebook with
evil relish, the traffic warden.

5. *Extension*, the opposite of 4 and by far the commonest
   process, whereby the original word-sense gathers additional meanings. Straightforward examples of extension
   like *earthing* a terminal are easily found. *Pin* has spread
   from the sense of a small pin, as in needlework, to
   many other meanings, e.g. the metal projection connected to the electrode which plugs into the holder. In
   textiles, *shoddy* (waste from a carding machine) gave
   the corresponding adjective meaning 'poor, tattered'.
   Or, to take a fishing example, the word *coble* was
   introduced to Withernsea on the East Yorkshire coast
   from Flamborough, a little farther north. Previously the
   local word was *crab boat*. Even though the Flamborough cobles have a square stern and the Withernsea
   boats a round one, the label *coble* has been transferred.

   It is true that, in contrast to the general meanings of
words, their scientific meanings, once established, rarely
change. But quite a number of words now have both general
and technical meanings. Sometimes extension brings technical terms into popular speech: thus *allergic* ('He's allergic to
redheads'); and *psychedelic*, originally applied to drugs
producing very vivid sensations but now to things like
flamboyant wallpaper. So words of this type have to be used
carefully. *Respiration* to the layman may mean simply the
process of breathing oxygen in and out; but the biological
sense, which includes the carrying of oxygen by blood to the
cells, is more complicated. Metals as well as people suffer
fatigue. Oil can crack, through reduction in the length of its
molecules, though the layman might think the oil expert
cracked to talk like that. Other terms with both general and
technical meanings (if in doubt, consult a dictionary) are:
*acid, alcohol, baffle, balance, density, frequency, governor,
neutral, obtuse, precipitate;* and even *berry* and *fruit*.
   Word meanings hold many traps. For instance, the same
word may have widely different technical meanings. *Jigger*,
besides its nautical meanings of a small tackle, a small
sail, a short mast and a type of sailing-smack, has stood for a

shoemaker's tool, a small notched wheel to cut pastry, a lathe used in making pottery, and an illicit distillery.* General words are not always trouble-free either. Around Blackburn, whatever the weather, if you *camp in th' woods* you need no tent but just *the gift of the gab*, for *camp* there means 'to chat'. In Standard English *simple* and *soft* can be used dispassionately, but on factory floors they are very emotive words meaning 'foolish'. *Call* can mean 'to scold', *starved* not hungry but very cold ('I feel right starved without mi topcoat'), and *funny* not 'laughable' but 'awkward', 'peculiar' or 'troublesome'. Because of the reactions they provoke, these words need care.

Differences of meaning can be quite involved. A *bun* in the North of England is a cake mixture; but the South produces *Chelsea bun* and *Bath bun*, which are quite different. *Pikelet* is used in the West and Midlands for a round teacake with small holes, to be buttered and toasted; but in other districts it seems to be a sticky unsweetened crumpet or else a muffin. If in doubt consult the ladies, for they are the experts here.

Changes of meaning can be curious. *Stick* is now a popular word for objects not made of wood. It can stand for giant electrodes made of iron, or the long-distance lorry-driver's gear lever — e.g. 'Coming down Shap, I knocked the bloody stick out'. This action is illegal, as it loses control of the vehicle, but the movement of meaning is not. A sharper instance is the Workington steelworks term *tin* for a paper bag weighed with 25 lb. of manganese, still so called because the chemical was once supplied in a tin! After this nothing should be a surprise. You won't turn a hair at *I've been to Traffic* (the transport controller's office); *self-clearing cafeterias* where actually the diners have to replace their trays after use; *are you a dinner?*, i.e. staying for dinner (no cannibalism intended); or at *newsboys, brew-boys* and *can-lads* who can all, despite their names, be fully-grown men. And everybody seems to realise that, when you boil the kettle, you are thinking of the water inside it.

Of course, change of meaning cannot be blamed where the speaker has confused the word. Unfamiliar ones are liable to

*See EDD *jigger*, sb., senses 5, 6, 9.

be distorted. In the pioneer days of motoring, electricity was sometimes mistakenly but aptly called *electrickery*; and when psychoanalysis was less known the psychiatrist could turn into the *trick-cyclist*. Similar is the patients' common mispronunciation *bronical asthma*. Many words when first encountered are so new as to be pronounced quite differently by different people. The first *i* of micriobiology is said both short and long, though one would expect the latter (*micro-*) to distinguish the micro-science from biology as a whole. *Fungi* is heard with six pronunciations — with 'hard' or 'soft' *g*; and with the *i* short, long and rhyming with *I*, or long and rhyming with *be*. Also the Latin suffixes *-ae* and *-i*, common in so many scientific words, are found being pronounced similarly, although this would distress any teacher of Latin.

Awkward mouthfuls give rise to common variants like *sithers* for scissors, *chimley, admirality, obstrokolus* for very hard to deal with (obstreperous), *he was absolutely parlatic* (i.e. paralytic, too drunk to stand). Very occasionally words are also distorted by spoonerisms, where their starts are interchanged. This is caused by rapid speech and thinking of words ahead, e.g. *spy and puds* for pie and spuds, *bend that mike* for mend that bike. *Din-opposed tweezle*, however, for twin-opposed diesel appears rather more suitable because that engine makes a great noise.

Sometimes corruption has been helped by folk etymology, where the speaker supplies an imagined source for the word from what it seems to say; e.g. *screwmatics* (rheumatism), *sparrow-grass* (asparagus). Popular etymology is at work too behind believers in *horrorscopes*, and a few others who seriously claim that *bungalow* comes, not as dictionaries insist from an Indian word, but from a poor builder who happened to *bungle* by making a house too *low*.

Worse still are malapropisms, named from Mrs. Malaprop, the character in Sheridan's *The Rivals* who was constantly confusing one word with another. The fact that people find the mistakes of Hilda Ogden in *Coronation Street* and Nellie Pledge of *Nearest and Dearest* so amusing suggests that they are not so daft as not to recognise a malapropism when they hear one. Yet, although it is always risky for employees to attempt words beyond them, they keep doing it, e.g.: 'We're working in collision'; 'this chemical's insolvent'; 'working women are getting too emaciated'; 'what our union feller said to the boss was inflammable'; 'when he decided to retire, they gave him a momentum'. Football provides more — e.g. of a player who took a fast low corner-kick, 'He was hoping for a rickshaw' (ricochet). More general malapropisms that have been heard include: 'We crossed the Channel by hoovercraft'; 'She's always incinerating'; 'our Sally's quite uninhabited'; 'he's a certified (certificated) teacher'; 'you have a very imaginary mind'; 'I can't do that, I'll be ostrichised'; 'I was left-handed but now I'm ambiguous'; 'I'm going to have electrocution lessons from a speech professor' (statement attributed to an Arsenal player); 'our lad's marrying a typewriter'; 'he bought it off a lady in seduced circumstances'.

Even learned societies, or their typists, can create apparent malapropisms — 'We hear that you are likely to postphone your application till next year' (from a British Academy letter). But easily the most fertile source of them is the doctor's waiting room, where patients try to grapple with names of illnesses they don't fully understand: 'I got determinitis and they insulated me for a week'; 'culinary thrombosis'; 'very coarse veins'; 'the doctor says it's infla-tion'; 'I was very confiscated, so they gave me an enemy'. *Shop-stupid* for a shop-steward is surely in a different category because it is deliberate. Most malapropisms, how-ever, are serious embarrassments to avoid if at all possible, because listeners secretly smile at them.

Some apparent mistakes cannot be helped. We should never blame laymen for not being experts. Where, for example, the *brook-ousel*, normally a blackbird, turns out to be a lapwing, there is no need to grow excited; or where the *jack-sharp*, usually a stickleback, becomes the *fish miller's thumb*, to go raving mad. Not many farmers or fishermen are biologists.

The same thing happens with the miner's terms for sedimentary rocks in the coal measures, which provide a bewildering variety of names. To take just one example of an approximate rock type, fireclay may be *cat, clod, clump, clunch, daugh, dawk, duns, gubbins* (what expressive names!), besides *seat-clay, seat-earth, seggar, sod, spavin, thill, underclay, warrant* and *warren-earth*. Again, the scientific inaccuracy of some of these terms is similar, because the ordinary miner can hardly be expected to be a geologist.

It is all right for botanists, with over 300,000 Latin and Greek names for species and genera at their disposal, but to a farmer couch grass is *twitch* or *wick* or whatever his ancestors have called it, and that is the end of the matter. The difficulties of conveying exact meaning are not fully realised. The factory hand, released from his bench to go fishing and ignorant of Latin and Greek, will not start bandying about classical words, but locally will call a parr, which is a salmon no more than a finger long, a *branlin, laspring, locksper, peel, rink, samlet, Samson* (emotive name!), *sil, skegger* or *skirling.* Just take your pick. This parr, or whatever you choose to call it, later becomes a silvery fish, usually termed a *smalt*, when a physiological change occurs in its body, allowing it to go from fresh to salt water. However, the time this happens varies, at age 1–2 years in Southern England but at 2–3 years in the Cheshire River Dee, bringing more linguistic doubt. The best thing is to listen to what your workmate says; make sure you understand what *he* means by it, and rest content.

There is one great comfort: context helps. The light engineer would be both idiotic and rash to blow (literally) his *trumpet*, for it is a smallish piece of apparatus into which molten metal might just have been *teemed*; a hospital patient, hearing of the *theatre*, won't be hoping to attend someone else's live show; and a *perm* at the hairdresser's is not for scooping the football pools. *Runners* speed on in athletics but not in building, where, e.g. they are pieces of wood nailed across ceiling joists; a *noggin* in a pub can be held upright as it is drunk, but in building it is a strut which is horizontal; a textile *jobber*, who is a young man who does odd jobs for the *underlooker*, oiling the machinery, mending belts and so on, would feel lost attempting the work of his namesake on the Stock Exchange. Relevant here is the story of the sub-postmaster who became annoyed about the man writing long letters in his busy shop. 'But I bought the envelopes and stamps here', protested the man. 'Look, mate', was the reply, 'we also sell lipsticks and laxatives.' Clearly, a great safety factor in word meanings, as in actions, is the context.

5 Sounds, Grammar and Style

It would be too much to ask the British workman to acquire just the same speech sounds as his neighbour, or to choose and link his words in just the same way. It would be as bad as asking him to wear exactly the same clothes, dye his hair the same colour, or eat identical meals. In fact, differences can be so wide that it is quite an achievement for the South--Westerner who says *oi baint* not to be puzzled or upset by the Bradford equivalent *I aren't* or those from other parts of England where they rejoice in declaring *I ammat, I aint, am nut* or *az nod*. Let's start with sounds, for they cause plenty of dissension.

Is it, for instance, *resin* or *rosin*, *duplicate* (as most of us believe) or, as some office-workers would have it, *dupplicate*? In fruits, is it *currant* or *corran; awmond, ahmond*, or *al* (like *pal*)-*mound*? Each has its adherents. To work it out, you need a clear head — or is it *eead, eyd, yerd* or *yed*? Good Gawd!

Two opposite processes can affect sounds. Extra ones may be inserted, like the unorthodox consonants in *chimbley, carnder* (corner), *parlder* (parlour), or the additional vowels next to *l* or *r* in *ath-a-letics, ellam* (for the tree or part of a ship's steering apparatus), *fillam, umberella* and *Stockollam tar*. Or by the opposite process sounds may be squeezed out — consonants, as in *thunner* (thunder) and *wunnerful*; vowels either initially as in *prentice* (apprentice), *cos* (because) and *tice* (entice), or medially as in *plice* (police) and *Satdy* (Saturday), or consonant and vowel as in *scaffling* (scaffolding). This type of shortening is branded vulgar and *iggorant*. Yet, though it is much commoner on the shop-floor than in accepted English, it is nothing new, having given us many standard words like *sport* from *disport, squire* from *esquire, Leicester*, and so on.

A third process is that a sound may change, almost beyond recognition. Incredible as it may seem, there are parts of

England where the farmer ploughs his *foorth* (furrow), where
the sow begins to *farth* (farrow), to produce, naturally, a
farth litter; and where there are *fleffs* or *flecks* instead of
fleas. *Keighley* in Yorkshire and the older pronunciation
Layth for Leigh in Lancashire include modern attempts (in
the sound *th*) at the old guttural ∠X∠ which dropped out of
spoken Standard English, but survives in our *gh* spellings
straight, right, weigh, etc., and all the changed-sound examples of this paragraph. It is still possible to find farmers up on
the Pennines between Burnley and Hebden Bridge who in
natural conversation distort an occasional word with a
guttural, e.g. by saying *Switch t'leyght* (light) *on*.

Sometimes the experienced hand can be recognised when
he sounds words in a way special to his occupation. Thus on
the English canal system the wide ponds constructed at
convenient intervals to let commercial craft turn easily are
winnding holes to the old professional boatman, not *winding
holes* as the modern canal enthusiast 'correctly' calls them. In
the Royal Navy and with old fishermen, boat seats are
usually *thawts*, not *thwarts*; tackle is *taykle* or *taygle*; and
launch is often *lahnch*.

Don't, however, believe all you hear. Wild claims have been
made for certain sounds — that words like *pig* and *stupid* have
from their sounds alone an insulting tone, that the vowels in
cool and *calm* are soothing, that the short rounded *oo*-sound
coming twice in the Northerner's *mud and blood* is ugly. But
this last vowel is similar to that in Standard English *pull,
push*, etc.; and sounds are themselves neither beautiful nor
ugly, neither vulgar nor snobbish, but just sounds.

Official technical language, especially that of electro-
communications (e.g. *teeter-totter* for a scanning array), likes
alliteration; and industrial workers show an even greater
fondness for alliteration and rhyme. Compare 'I'll love you
and leave you', with 'to swap and cop' (give and take), 'toil
and moil (to work hard). This must be because throughout
our language's history, from the age of the Anglo-Saxon
minstrels onwards, the chief aids to memory have been
alliteration or rhyme.

Stress — linguistic besides psychological — is another
feature of industrial language. Asking at the works canteen

for *a napple* or *a negg* is caused by inability to detect the phonetic boundaries between words. Other cases of irregular stress come from not realising what the most important part of a word is. The main stress may be put too late, as very commonly in main*tain*ance (said, not spelt, like that) or 'It's an Admir*a*lity job'; or else too early, as in *horrizon* or the frequent pronunciation *ree-search*. Strange that researchers of all people should want to stress the *re-* or 'back' element instead of the progressive idea of *search*!

The strangest stressing at present, in view of its origin, often comes from television news commentators who keep over-stressing the wrong words, so partly destroying their meaning. This is amazing, since with less educated speakers it would imply that they don't know what on earth they are talking about. The regular B.B.C. news-readers rarely do this but the commentators often do (e.g. 'Mr Whitelaw went on a walk-*about*', for '... *walk*-about'). Listen to them, and, unless they have suddenly mended their ways, you will find what is meant.

Linked with stress is unusual voicing, partly because of a particular occupation. The so-called 'clahgyman's voice' is because the cleric has to be heard all over his church, often with poor acoustics. The sergeant-major barks short high-pitched commands by suddenly jerking inwards his stomach muscles, and does so to bring from his squad sharp and immediate responses. Beginners on school practice often suffer from 'student-teacher's throat', hoarseness from over-exertion of the throat muscles, for which the cure is relaxation (so far as this is possible before a noisy class!) and speaking more from the diaphragm. Then there is station announcer's voice, releasing ghost vowels, like 'The train-a to York-a is now-a standing-a at number three-a platform-a'. We may smile at it, but at least it sounds more appropriate than if the announcement came, 'Th' train what gooas to York is now stood fer yer on platfooarm fower'. It is merely to be hoped that such people don't carry their professional voices home: it would be unwise for the vicar to deliver a full-blown sermon at breakfast to his wife, or for the sergeant-major by brisk commands to make his spring to attention. Similarly, if the station announcer back at home proclaimed, 'I-a still-a await-a my tea-a', there would be an unusual household reaction.

History, that of regional accents, is a second reason for unusual voicing. The typical Bradford native is recognised by his pronunciation *Bratford* with insufficient voice; but over-voicing is also common, especially west of the Pennines. A remarkable case — so far as is known, the only one just like it in the world — occurred till at least fifteen years ago in the speech of shrimpers near Southport, who unconsciously through heavy voicing put an *n* or *m* on the ends of words. Thus a bag would become a *bag-n*; a pig, *pig-n*; a church, *church-m*. Frequent still over South Lancashire is *gazz* for gas and *buzz* for bus. The story runs that the Lancashire worker, shopping in the West End, asked a Londoner, 'Wheer do ah catch th' buzz?' 'Don't you mean the bus, my man?' the pedant queried. 'Ah should know what they're called', came the reply, 'Ah come fra Leyland, wheer we mek 'em'.

Grammar is just as interesting. Though it is scarcely limited to any occupation or group of occupations, workmen cannot talk without it. Noteworthy are frequent usages like *no hammer nor nowt*, a treble negative once possible in Standard English;* *without* (unless) *we go*; *they fun* (found) *it*; *ah clum* (climbed) *up*; *there's nee men gan in there* ('there are no men going in there', with *who* omitted); and *a bit fluff*, a North-Eastern usage without *of*. Other examples are *some on* (of) *'em*; *'e done* (did) *it*; *uzsen* (ourselves), a Midland feature contrasting with Northern *uzsell*; the weird double plurals *bellowses* 'pair of bellows' and *gallowses* 'braces'; and *off of it* 'off it', a South-Eastern feature but now spreading north. These singularities aren't just the concern of the grammarian, nor should they be. The press made great play of some extraordinary delays at a level-crossing on the Scarborough line, where a notice stated, 'Wait while the trains pass'. Puzzled Yorkshiremen, to whom *while* means 'until', waited and waited. . .

In spoken industrial language, the prepositions *on* and *of* are frequently confused. There is a joke about a newcomer to

---

*Cf. Chaucer's description of the Knight in his Prologue to *The Canterbury Tales*: 'He never yet no villainie ne'er said . . .'.

the gang approaching his mates with an empty *baccy* pouch and asking, 'As any on yer any on yer?', to which the answer comes, 'None on us 'as none on us'. There are practically no present-participle constructions, unlike formal written English: 'Inspecting the pump, I detected a leak' would become 'When I looked at . . .' And there are more one-word sentences, with subject and verb understood, like 'Morning', 'Spade!', 'Here, you!' Some of these grammatical usages are also dialectal or regional, but since they are quite evident in occupational speech cannot be ignored.

Closer inspection of occupational grammar brings other things to light. Before the names of diseases and illnesses, many workmen use *the* in defiance of Standard English; e.g. 'I've getten *the* rheumatics/flu/fever' or 'He's got *the* ditherum shacks' (tremors). *The* is strongly preferred to *my* in *the missus*, and to *our* in *the boss*, perhaps because the employee thinks they are not his property like his dog or clothes as he can't do what he likes with them. But at the other extreme *the* quite disappears from the speech of some Hull dockers, who say, e.g. *Pur it into van* (not even *t' van* or *th' van*). This remarkable omission is a feature of East Riding talk, especially also around Patrington.

With gender, we have outgrown the ridiculous older English idea of classifying *fishing* as masculine, *strength* as feminine and *child* as neuter; but in works language gender has not quite disappeared. Countries, when thought of as localities, are *it*, but as fictitious persons (*Wales, the motherland*) are usually *she*. Cities and factories, being often unfriendly and hostile, are *it*. In transport, trains and aircraft are usually *it*, sometimes *she*; cars are usually *it*, but when they run very sweetly *she*; whilst unnamed small craft like punts and dinghies are *it*, but watercraft with sail or power *she*.

A few people seem to change sex. A *Meg-Harry* is a soft-voiced effeminate man, and a *Mary-Ann* is one who helps his wife unduly with housework, shopping and children. This is because when not at work, even when out of work, the working-class man rarely helped his wife. It was seemingly accepted that wives were there for bed, child-bearing, cleaning, cooking, shopping, keeping accounts straight and supervising children. In workaday language, gender has an emotional rather than a grammatical or biological meaning.

Here and there, nouns are unusual. Unchanged plurals like *two foot/mile/gallon* are supposed to be from preserving the old genitive plural after numbers (e.g. Old English *twēo fōta*, 'two of feet'). *Two foot*, etc., now seem idiomatic, probably because they are much-used workmen's phrases often heard by the public; whereas e.g. *2 mile 1 inch*, a rare length, is not idiomatic. There is variation. Many Northerners, even educated ones, say e.g. *four foot* but *120 feet*. Then, for ownership of nouns, factory-floor language can develop some grotesque contortions, like *I'll go to Fisheses* (Fish's shop) or *'er as I go out with's mother*.

Many wayward pronouns feed on factory language: remembering that pronouns are not out-of-the-way erudite expressions but common linking words vital to all speech, we might wonder whether many a worker ever went to school, unless it was a grammar school for dialect. A speaker seems to show a split personality in saying *Give us* ('me') *it*. *Thou* and *thee* are frequent when talking to equals or inferiors, but not to authority. A work-mate called *thou great gawp!* might accept it, not exactly as an endearment, but without too much fuss as a run-of-the-mill hazard; but to say it to the foreman or the boss would be the height of insolence, increased by the *thou*. The South and South-West love *'n* for 'him' or 'it', as in *get 'n done*; Norfolk and Irish workers employ *yous* for the plural 'you'. 'She' in the North Midlands is sometimes *shoo* and with elderly Lancashire folk *hoo*.* Both are confusing. *Shoo* may remind you of cobbling; and the first time I met *hoo* was in a lifeboat house, where the old salt suddenly uttered *Hoo's gooin' out*. Startled, I thought it was a question, but his gestures then showed he was referring to the Isle of Man boat sailing up the channel.

Technically speaking, we often get objective for subjective. In other words, you find e.g. *Him and me did it, Them as* ('those who') *left that muck ought to be shot*, or *'Who said that?' 'Her!'* Also, an unnecessary pronoun often slips in, e.g.

*OE *hēo*.

That bloke, he's an inspector. This way of using an additional pronoun was not unknown in Anglo-Saxon times.

Only the individualistic Irish seem over-fond of *-self*, using it for emphasis instead of ordinary personal pronoun (*It's myself that did it*). In England it is commoner to find the opposite, too little *-self* and too much *me*, in reflexive uses like 'I'll sit me down', 'I'm learning me a new job', 'I'll bethink/change/dress/wash me'.

Many changes are rung amongst relative pronouns. Examples are: *'im as* (or *at* or *what*) *I've knowed*; or *I know a man'll get yer one*, without the expected *who*. Of indefinite pronouns, *'un* keeps cropping up as in *that's a rotten 'un*; but *owt, nowt* and *summat* also make their presence felt. A Yorkshire cheesemaker, asked at a Board of Trade investigation what he thought of their wartime plan to reorganise cheesemaking and cheese distribution in his dale, answered *Nowt!*, and reckons that that one expressive word swayed the official mind far more than many an eloquently phrased sentence would have done. The resilience of these unorthodox pronouns is shown by a number of current proverbs, like:

> Hear all, see all, say nowt,
> Eat all, sup all, pay nowt

and by arguments like 'Then as has nowt, is nowt. If they'd had owt, they'd a' bin summat'. There is no need to laugh at the workman's use of this trio. Like *thou* and *thee*, they are well established in older and Biblical English, and equal *aught, naught* and *somewhat*.

For pointing out, the industrial worker may so far forget himself as to use consistently the Standard English demonstratives *this, that, these* and *those*; but he is more likely to deviate, e.g. into *this here, that there*, or for distant things *yon*; or sometimes in the West Country to the peculiar *thicky* and *thacky*; or anywhere in England to *them* for those (*them plugs*). If such wide disagreement persists over these ordinary terms, what hope is there that everyone will come to understand detailed scientific language?

For intensifying, the human cog of industry uses a whole kit of linguistic tools without hesitation. One way is to use two adjectives of kindred meaning, such as *a little tiny bit*, or *a great big feller*; another is *that* for 'certainly' as in *Ay, they did, that.* Or he throws out at random any intensifier that takes his fancy from those in the following list: '*a rare/real/ mighty* good 'un', 'an *awful* lot', '*terrible* slow', '*mortal* big', 'a *proper* mix-up', or sarcastically 'a *right* mess!'

Other matters, trivial to the speaker and many hearers, but frustrating perhaps to the language enthusiast, include: *best* ('better') *of the two; I'll do it easy* ('easily'); *get wer tools* ('get our . . .', by changing the stress in *our*), or *get us tools*; and those unnecessary prepositions, notorious throughout the West Country but also found e.g. in Lakeland, as in *Where's he to?* ('Where is he?'), *Where's that hat at?* New managements might consider safeguarding themselves by appointing, after those essential people, competent accountants, a works interpreter!

All this time we haven't breathed a word about verbal forms, although some Standard English ways of using them are very foreign to the factory floor. Official report language, like 'Putting his hand into the machinery, he lost a finger', becomes in shop-floor English 'When he put . . .'. Verb endings themselves are curious, and an interesting test could be made on the following lines:

1. Give the Standard English equivalents of the following interrogatives: *Ista?, Asta?, Canta?, Wilta?, Dusta?*
2. Comment on the sense or otherwise of: *Oh you was, was you?; they lays* (= lay) *on t' top; the lads goes* (= go) *fishing.*
3. Translate: *I clum upstairs, fun mi watch, an' wun it up.*
4. How aesthetic are these past tenses and past participles? — *it shrunk, stunk and then sunk; I've took it and shook it; he's letten 'em put 'etten' where they should a' putten 'getten'.*
5. In five minutes, cut the tails off as many verbs as you can, like this: *It's bin tore/wore/swore/froz . . .*
6. In another five minutes, if you have strength and heart left, extend as many others as possible as sometimes in works English, like this: *he's getten throwed* ('got thrown') *out; it was hitten and then drownded . . .*

Such cases are not as idiotic as they seem. For example, in sets 3—6 above analogy, reasoning from parallel cases, has been at work. And we musn't take our fun too far. Though on paper the examples look comical, they don't usually sound so. Similarly, in considering those comical but genuine advertisements like *experienced lady punch operator* or *boy wanted for butchering*, we must keep a sense of reality. There is no incitement to violence because the context makes all clear. Unusual sounds and grammar are intriguing, but they don't tell the whole story.

Scientific written style seems more difficult to analyse. Just as there is no ideal general English style, suitable for both formal and informal letters and all other occasions, so there is no perfect, all-embracing scientific style. The stylistic merits of any piece of writing depend on how far it fulfils its purpose. Here are short examples of very different scientific styles:

(*a*) 'If an appropriate electrical potential is applied across the opposite faces of crystal substances like quartz, Rochelle salt, or lead-zirconite-titanate, the crystal will become distorted in shape' (textbook writing, from E. Hughes, *Electrical Technology*).

(*b*) 'Under normal conditions a quantity of hydrogen gas will consist of many millions of these atoms linked in pairs, which are very stable and rather resemble a husband and wife combination, going through life together and only separating when the physical or chemical provocation is fairly violent' (very popular exposition to laymen).

(*c*) 'The E.A.S. corresponding to 270 kts. I.A.S. are below those corresponding to the V.N.O. given in D.H./C.A.A./1 for all altitudes up to 31,000 ft. T.P.A.' (communication amongst specialists).

Nevertheless, almost all scientific style has certain characteristics. Any trace of humour, bitterness, satire, climax, assonance or alliteration, all of which would distract from the impersonal message, is avoided. Vivid comparisons, except very occasionally for popular explanations like (*b*) above, are not indulged in. The scientist, fearful of inaccuracy, ruthlessly cuts out any hint of excitement or exaggeration. If his experiment bursts into a fantastic sight of bubbling frenzied gas, he may coldly report 'a copious effusion of nitrogen peroxide'; if agonised by a sudden electric shock, he may later impersonally admit 'an accidental earthing occurred'. At work, the scientist seems to lack the warmth of common humanity. His style may be effective enough for immediate purposes, but hardly beyond.

6 Bluntness and Friendliness

Occupational language can be a defence. Like a dialect, slang or the favourite words of any community, it stresses the group's solidarity and warns outsiders to keep away. There is something friendly about it, however, for members of the group. A young worker who would resent being called an idiot will take less exception to being called *feckless; daft* or *gaumless*; he would object if his mates called him a long-haired lout but less if they labelled him a *woolly Derbyshire ram.*

There is no doubt about the language's bluntness, which comes out in all sorts of ways. Technical words used as needed generally make far greater impact than Standard English ones, whatever the occupation. This applies even to gardening, where e.g. *bloomy down* is a vivid term for the sweet william and *dodman* another just as striking for a garden snail. The experienced workman tends to lose patience with ignorant outsiders who can't understand. This was delightfully shown at Worcester Assizes,* where a witness in a case kept referring to a field full of *oonty-tumps*. The judge, a townsman, was severely puzzled by this, as illustrated by the following exchanges:

Judge: 'What are these oonty-toomps you keep mentioning?'
Witness: 'What be oonty-toomps? They be the toomps the oonts make'.
Judge: 'But what are oonts?'
Witness: 'Why them as makes the toomps'.

It might help to know here that *oonty-toomps* are actually molehills.

Official English is full of hackneyed expressions which are not necessarily wrong but which through over-use have lost much of their meaning — recent offenders include *high-level,*

*G. L. Brook, *English Dialects.*

57

top secret, denigrate and now *viable* — but industrial language has no such problem. This is not to say that shops, offices and factories don't harbour some platitudes and wishful thinking ('You can only die once', 'It'll all be over by Christmas'). Ritual in words and actions does intervene there to some extent, e.g. in making a purchase or in the common *thank you very much*; but it is not so marked. There is less of the polite formulae of disengagement ('It's been so nice to see you' or the deliberately vague 'We must meet again some time'), and certainly less of the negative use of language to hide the truth or frustrate inquiry, so essential apparently to the politician or the bureaucrat. Workers feel quite free to discuss a colleague or the merits of their local football team without the rigmarole of a polite formula. It is not, 'Did you observe Hurst's well-taken goal?' but 'Geoff Hurst fair hit a smasher, didn't he?'.

It doesn't follow that, because of its plainness and bluntness, occupational language is without abstract nouns. Indeed it has some far more vivid than their Standard English counterparts. Although it is an abstract word of Greek origin, *nous*, as in *He's got no nous* ('sense'), hardly sounds Greek or foreign at all on the shop floor when spat out behind a workmate's back. *Gumption* for commonsense, and *guts* and *spunk* for bravery or determination, also sound concrete and realistic enough. Yet another is *bant* for strength or endurance — 'He's got some bant in him'.

The outspoken nature of industrial language is confirmed by the sheer mass of words for unfortunate personal characteristics and habits. A person isn't just foolish — he may be branded *daft, feckless, thick, dozy, potty, muzzy, mopy, simple, sapless, gommy* or *dateless*; or else he is very likely a *dummel-head, bluffin-head, bowster-yed, barm-yed, chewter-eead, clot, feather-yed, blockhead, numskull, gowk* or *gawk* (originally a cuckoo or an apple core!), *silly gobbin* or *cow-yed*. The last is supposed to come from the label given by neighbouring Boltonians to the Westhoughton farmer who, finding his cow stuck in a five-barred gate, to free it cut off his head, although Westhoughton residents claim that the whole point of his action was that it was a Westhoughton gate that was being damaged.

Anything unusual or comical always stands out, and, judging by the wide relevant vocabulary, industrialists must have to put up with a weird assortment of employees. Many of them are from time to time, though not strictly drunk, certainly *drukken, druffen, bottled, sozzled, fuddled, kettled, tight, half seas under, bevvied, palatic* (corruption of *paralytic*), or *pissed* or *half-pissed* (for uncouth language, see Chapter 11). When this happens, they don't talk nonsense but *rubbish, kelt, tommy rot* or *double Dutch*. Although they are not clumsy, their efficiency is affected when, as sometimes, they are known to be *butter-fingered, awkward, clumbersome, numb-pawed*, or *thumby*.

Very few workpeople are left-handed but it is not unusual to notice that a colleague is *kay-pawed, cuddy-wifted, dolly-posh, bang-handed, back-handed* (not here in order to accept a tip!), *keggy* or *kaggy*. Fortunately their hair never seems to get tangled, which might be dangerous near unguarded machinery; though it easily becomes *matted, cottery, knotted, luggy, pluggy, tousled, rough, ruffled, fuzzy* or *towy*. They rarely get dirty; but often *clarty, mucky* or *muck-shot*.

At work, people's physical states tend to be a little abnormal. You are not well, but *in good nick, shape, trim* or *fettle*; not ill, but *not so good, nobbut middlin'* or *sick* — without vomiting, which doesn't happen anyway because instead you would *puke* or *spew*. You are not weak, but *feeling dicky, wankly, wangled, wammy, groggy, waffled* or *keggly*.

Objects can be abnormal too. For instance, nothing made at work is recognisably repaired, though it may be *codged up* or *fiddled*; nothing results from mistake or error, though e.g. London postmen admit to occasional *drop-offs*; nothing can be spoilt or ruined, though admittedly it may be *gash, frigged, botched, dud, duff* or *fallen down*. The last can apply e.g. to an electrical mechanism which has failed its test and to a workman, but in the latter sense should not be taken literally — 'He's fallen down on the job' doesn't mean that he has tripped and fallen headlong.

Food becomes *bait, budgy* (not the bird), *grub, jock, meat, peck, snap* or *tommy*, and contrasts oddly with officialese.

When in a recent T.V. disucussion under David Dimbleby an official was explaining food's calorific value, a worker butted in with 'I bet you don't have to put marge on your snap'; and the language helped to show that worker and official belonged to different worlds. Miserly habits are common, judging by the number of *nip-cheeses, nip-farthings, nip-raisins, scrimps* and *skinflints. Nip-raisin* was actually a true description of a Bolton grocer who was infamous for making sure he gave as little weight as possible. Few gossips are encountered; but you will meet many, especially amongst the ladies, who are allegedly *clat-cans* because they are always e.g. *calling, camping* (not in fields) or *chin-wagging.* Very particular or capricious people shouldn't be so described in a works, where it would hardly mean a thing; but at your disposal are suitable alternatives like *chancy, faddy, giddy kippers, kysty,* or the long description *you never know when you've got him.*

Violence stands out anywhere, and the hoped-for peace of industrial relations must often be disturbed as one ferocious-looking fellow threatens to *do, bash, baste, beat, belt, flay, lam, lambaste, paste, skelp, wallop* or *tan the hide off* his opponent; and, perhaps, not even to make the other man agree, but only so that he will *side with* him. Or he may draw from his repertoire other threats of physical violence, like *I'll gi' thee thi bats, I'll bensill/nevill/bray you, I'll gi' thee a clout over t'head, I'll lace your jacket.* And many workers greet you automatically with *Now then!*, as if you have been guilty of something. After all these blunter alternatives you probably feel exhausted; but not ordinary working mortals, who just become *dead beat, mafted, pagged, powfagged, shot* or *absolutely buggered.* Friendly the language may well be but, before he realises that, the stranger is due for many a shock.

7 Animals and People

Industrial vocabulary contains a fine collection of animals, with specimens more remarkable than those in Standard English or the zoos. People are given animal names, of which a few are affectionate, like *lamb, pet* or *duckie* (all women's terms) but most are hostile. Depending on just how you are thinking at the time, a person you have to work with may be an *ape, ass, bitch, daft old donkey, cow, old crow, clacking hen, goose, cuckoo, elephant, pig, toad, rat, swine, worm, shark, skunk*, and so on. Other animal names show amused tolerance; notably *little monkey* for a mischievous youngster (*Right, monkey* being common long before Al Reed popularised it), *old dog, sly old fox* and *butterfly*.

Far more often, in order to make work surroundings seem more friendly, objects rather than people are allotted animal names. This helps especially to bring giant things down to a smaller homelier size. Thus we meet *jumbo* for the giant jet-plane or for an enormous tank into which steel is poured, and *spider* for a great circle of turbine blades.

Altogether a wide range of animals is let loose in industry. If only a few wild man-eating ones could be imported, there would be no need to leave our towns and cities for Longleat or Knowsley to find a great safari park. In the steelworks a *bear* is a piece of metal left in the well of a furnace; a *monkey*, a small bar fastened to a ladle; a *dog*, a mechanical device with teeth and claws for grabbing ingots; *pigs*, lengths of pig-iron; and *sows*, large channels of molten metal from which the pigs run and are so 'born'. The last idea is taken over in distillation, where the apparatus for separating distillation fractions is known as the *sow* (or sometimes through mishearing *cow*) and the tubes leading from it are the *pigs*.

Down the mine, too, there are *dogs* and *monkeys*, these being gadgets used in securing various items of machinery in the pit; and, though we don't usually consider a mine as agricultural territory, it rears *bulls*, which are pieces of iron attached to the roof and which drop onto the track after the tubs have passed; and *cows*, a name given to the iron shackles connecting tubs.

In building, a course of *pig* occurs where the heights of different layers of bricks meeting at a corner do not correspond. Then on the permanent way every railway wagon has a name — *salmon* for a long type, *plaice, flat-fish*, etc. These were named, not from their colours and shapes, but from a code given years ago by pure chance. And presumably almost everyone reading of the Stock Exchange has heard of its *bulls, bears* and *stags*, though sadly most investors won't easily admit what or whom these animals feed on!

A smallish animal which seems to have grown enormous is the *Mersey mole*, the giant excavator used to make the second Mersey tunnel. Very small animals met in industry include the *mouse*, for putting in sash windows and consisting of a piece of string to which a weight is attached; the *flea*, a general laboratory word for a little piece of metal used in magnetic stirring; *beast* (i.e. a very small one) for a biological specimen; and *bugs*. This last can stand for the whole bacteriology department ('I work in bugs', 'Take this beast to bugs') as does *stinks* for the chemistry department. *Bugs* is also the computer programmer's method of passing the blame. It is a human failing not to admit mistakes, and computers are often still foolishly programmed. Therefore the programmer who has made the initial errors which cannot easily be taken out, will say on handing the work to a colleague, 'Watch it: it still has a few bugs in'.

The leisure industry accommodates animals too. The cricketer gets the occasional *duck*; the golfer obtains *birdies, eagles*, and if he is exceptional the rare *albatross* (respectively one, two and three under par); whilst the surf-riding novice may be able only to *chicken-ride* in fear, lying face-down. In ten-pin bowling we find the *turkey* for three stikes in a row. This could be a corruption of *thirty* but, since the game's complicated scoring prevents it always equalling that number, it may come just from the idea of something outstandingly good, just as turkey, reserved usually for Christmas, is thought the best meat.

The connection between animal names and the objects

they represent is usually strong, and applies wherever in industry the comparison is used. For example *dog*, besides the cases just mentioned, is used for the driving dogs in a lathe, the underlying idea being that a dog has a fierce bite. Sometimes quite different objects are given the same animal name because their similarities override any differences in function. Thus a *dog collar* is worn not only by a dog but by a vicar, though you wouldn't dream of attaching a lead to exercise a vicar. Sometimes the animal comparisons are vaguer, as in *monkey wrench* and *donkey jacket*. Here a slight connection might exist between the gripping power of the wrench and that of a monkey, and between the donkey, a hard-working beast of burden, and the type of jacket which is used by labourers and therefore has to stand up to much wear and tear. But here the language links are weak.

Animals enter many comparisons. This is because people have always had animals round them, as a source of friendship, or for meat and clothes; and so have been able to observe animal traits and their similarity to man's. *To go dogging* is to follow courters; whilst in electronics we find the *cat's whisker diode*, only doubtfully resembling a cat's whisker, on the roof we spy the *cat-walk*, and on the road at night *cat's-eyes*. Rushing late for work, we may give ourselves just a *cat-lick* or hasty wash, still with our feline friends; and, if our car is slow to accelerate, grumble that it *runs like a sick pig* (even a healthy pig takes some moving!). Others are: 'he squints like a basket o' whelps', 'as gawmless as a sucking duck', 'as hoarse as a cuckoo', 'to stare like a choked throstle', 'legs like a linnet' (very thin legs indeed), 'he's that bow-legged, he couldn't stop a pig in a snicket (= alleyway).'

But even animals in their usual surroundings acquire other names. The worker pursuing his weekend hobby of angling may find round a pond *cockies* or *jacksharps*, 'sticklebacks' to the uninitiated, and *bull-heads*, 'tadpoles' which turn into *paddocks*. Among insects we find *yedthers*, *attercrops* and *lops*, called respectively by dictionary-makers dragonflies, spiders and fleas. Then there are *orchans, foumarts, brocks, clocks,* and *mowdiwarps*, termed by those who know no better hedgehogs, polecats, badgers, broody hens and moles. In birds, starlings are *shepsthers*, sparrows *spadgers*, thrushes *throstles* or *trolleys*, crows are commonly *rooks* (compare Shakespeare's *Macbeth*, 'The crow makes wing to the rooky wood') fieldfares and redwings are *snowbirds*, yellow wagtails are *yollerseeds*; and, if you are told, 'You're as black as a brookousel (blackbird)', you badly need a wash.

People, besides animals, are brought into industrial language. Personification of workaday objects and surroundings is another way of relieving drabness and creating a friendly atmosphere. In the steel mills, the giant Bessemer converter is personified. It has a *nose*, from which come *snotters*, streams of metal dribbling from the ladles (if they solidify on the ladle they are *whiskers*), besides *jaws*, a *belly* and *kidneys*, whilst its apron is its *slagging breast*. The blast furnace too is personified, with its *throat* and *belly*. So is the ingot when, through being poured too slowly, it develops a surface crust known as *skull*.

Rocks have *faces*, rivers have *mouths*. Parts of the human body are used in naming machine parts, like the *head* of a bolt and a car distributor's rotor *arm*. Cars, besides being animalised when they *purr* along like docile cats, are personalised into females with *bonnets*. The baking industry uses *bonnet* for the handled lid covering a loaf when it is pushed into the oven, and another human expression there is *bucky dough* for dough exerting strong resistance, which resembles a Scottish word for an obstinate person.*

Fishing language has many personifications. The fisherman, in addition to telling his child to rub the dirty *tide-mark* off its unwashed neck, will speak of the *leg* for rope of a crab-pot, the *deadman* for a quayside iron bollard, the *foot* of a landing-stage, the *shank* (English) or *cois* (Welsh 'leg') of an anchor, the *ribs* of a ship or crab-pot, a *school* of porpoises, and so on. The ship is often personified. A trawler has a *ship's husband*, an agent 'married' to it while it is in port, one of whose important duties is to persuade drunken *deckies* (deckhands) to sail. A Fleetwood trawler skipper was quoted as waxing lyrical about his female ship's recovery from buffeting by a giant wave: 'The little beauty decided she did not want to go. What a wonderful ship! She came

*Cf. *OED*, *buckie*, Sc., 2.

back up, shook herself down and after that just laughed at those big bloody seas.'*

Human parallels are drawn in many other spheres. A railway *sleeper* looks immovable like someone soundly asleep. A stranger railway term is the *dumb buffer* for a springless one, because even a sprung one would not be expected to speak, so that it must have originated differently from the *dumb waiter*. Good examples of personification occur in the sporting occupation of bowling, which has the *blocker*, a wood sent deliberately short; ways of referring to a wood ('It's merry' if it goes too fast, or 'It's lost its way'); and the agonised antics of bowlers following their woods, by which they seem to be appealing to their protegés.

Sometimes the personification goes a step farther, to named persons. From the Great War came the long-range gun *Big Bertha*; and today we find many of them, like *Jack-of-all-trades*, *Johnny Dory* (the fish), *steeplejack*, a *plain Jane*, a *dandy* (from *Andrew*), a *peeping Tom*, a *smart Alec*, a *Sam Browne* (Army officer's belt and straps), a *Sally Lunn* (small light teacake), *jerry-builder*, and a *dismal Jonah*. Railway enthusiasts have been responsible for many personal names, e.g. *Nelson* for the London-to-Portsmouth train which had only one clear window at the front, the other showing the destination, and so resembling the British admiral blind in one eye; and the *Queen of Sheba*, not particularly long but of high capacity, reminiscent of the Biblical monarch who had 'a great train'.

As shown in Chapter 12, the electronics industry is very fond of making its abbreviations look like Christian names. There is, for example, a device for circuits nicknamed a *Lazy Susan*. Unfortunately a problem inherent in it is that it may take several days before its big and unwieldy apparatus is assembled, boring and frustrating the operator.† That is why the *Susan* is called *lazy*.

The devil is often personified, not only in the cliché *dark Satanic mills* but in the textile industry as the *devil*, a machine for tearing up cloth to be remade as shoddy, and in

---

Blackpool Evening Gazette, 13 November 1972.
† Cf. *Electronics Weekly*, 18 October 1972.

devil's dust, the flock that flew about during this process to the great discomfort of the workers. *Devils* were also the inky boys who helped qualified printers in their 'black art', and the term is frequent in legal circles where an assistant barrister is asked to *devil* for a better-known principal. Near Hallowe'en around Great Budworth in Cheshire, the farming community still enacts a quaint 'soul-caking' play (the *soul-cake* being a glass of beer or any sustenance the audience will provide for the ever-thirsty actors), into which comes the devil; but his name has changed from the unknown or unwanted *Beelzebub* to *Belshy Bob* or, befitting the pubs where the play is usually given, *Belcher Bob*.

Finding new words can be a problem, sometimes overcome by attaching a person's name to what is described. These coinages are nearly always applied to new ideas, products or discoveries, not just to rename already defined ones. *Pasteurisation* and *Mendelism* are good examples. It is easy to see that the *farad*, the unit of electrical capacity, comes from the great inventor Faraday, and the *maxwell*, the unit of magnetic flux, from the personal name. It is a popular way of solving the problem, as it increases the inventor's fame. But it should be used with discretion: an American palaeontologist once suggested the species *Hesperopithecus harold j. cookii* from a molar tooth discovered by a Harold J. Cook* How many derivations from famous people can you clearly work out from the following list? – ampere, bakelite, burberry, boycott, cardigan, dahlia, fuchsia, henry, hertz, guillotine, joule, macadam, mackintosh, mauser, ohm, shrapnel, talbot, volt, watt, weber, wellingtons.

Sometimes a tool acquires a personal name, as in the Nottinghamshire request *Pass us* ('me') *a Charlie Smith*, a wooden wedge nicknamed from a miner obsessed by its importance, who thought it was the repair answer to everything. To be immortalised like this, not by medal, statue or time-worn tombstone but on people's lips, is the height of fame. Industrial language is all the better for its references to animals and people.

*Hogben, p. 37.

8 Talking without Speaking

Sign language or non-verbal communication is another widespread and important characteristic of industrial language. It is used to show approval, enthusiasm, friendship or affection, to disagree, or to explain. As people converse, they unconsciously watch each other's gestures and eye movements, and are subtly influenced by them. We may, for instance, wink, nod our heads, shrug our shoulders or gesture with our hands. Communication comes through the five senses via sound (e.g. the jingling music of 'Workers' Playtime', alarm bells or buzzers), visual sensations (paintings, gestures, grimaces), tactile sensations (tugging a pal's sleeve to indicate curiosity, stroking hair, holding hands), smell (of tar, of burning clothing, of a freshly manured field), and taste (e.g. beer or a succulent meal).

So much non-verbal communication now exists that, knowing its pattern, we take most of it for granted. Clocks, picture advertisements and dials we often ignore; and huge roadside hoardings, maintained at great cost, we generally treat just as part of the landscape. This type of advertising is really the strangest in its results because it is seen by so many but remembered by so few — it may serve to keep in mind an established product but will not sell a new one. When driving, we tend automatically to obey traffic lights, arrows on the road and so on, having met so many of them before. Where some, like speed-limit signs and double yellow lines, are occasionally ignored, this is deliberate, not through ignorance; or else there are special circumstances, as with the woman driver, stuck at traffic lights and frantically trying to engage any gear, whom the policeman after rapping on her car roof sarcastically asked, 'Now, madam, have we no colour you prefer?'

Northerners are supposed to gesticulate more than Londoners because they are less articulate. Whether this is true has still to be proved, for the Northerner's words, when they do escape him, are certainly strong and clear. His *Belt up!* may not have the nuances of *Please desist* or *Kindly stop immediately*, but it hardly needs supplementing by a clenched fist, shaking the unfortunate hearer or other hostile action.

When the English workman uses gesture, it needs no translation. Disgust is clearly expressed by grimacing, frowning, pursing his lips, etc.; wonder by open mouth, wide-open eyes, etc., pleasure by smiling, chuckling or outright laughter; tension by crouching, or sitting gingerly on a chair edge; and so on. Nor is there any confusion between meaningful movements like those so far noted and the nervous tics and twitches of workpeople subject to overstrain, which are thought part of the current personalities of their unfortunate maker. Deceit is shown, for instance by averting the eyes; but honest industry has far less of this than polite social occasions, with their etiquette, conventional gestures and many white lies (e.g. 'Just what I wanted' — 'I don't think', 'Oh, I wouldn't say that' — 'At least, not to your face').

The business handshake suggests honesty. The first one you met may well have surprised you with its suddenness and firmness, but soon they become familiar. Their meaning is to seal a mutual bargain or, if you view it more cynically, 'That's to stop you getting out of it'.

Certain actions, like a nudge or placing the forefinger by the side of the nose, are thought decidedly vulgar, but even then context matters. After all, an itching side of your nose governs what you do to it; and the meaning of the Churchill victory-V sign differs fundamentally from its twin which indicates disgust.*

In industry, it is chiefly the working conditions that dictate the pattern of communication. Sign language is prevalent in noisy industries or those which require long-distance communication. The former type is found in textile mills and many factories, the latter is exemplified by the cricket umpire or semaphore.

In some very noisy industries, great use has to be made of sign language. In steelworks much of this has developed from

_____

*Named from a well-known user of this sign, the term *to do a Harvey Smith* has just reached the dictionaries.

the personification, mentioned in the previous chapter, of the Bessemer converter. Here is a selection from that industry's phrase-book:

Sign	*Meaning*
Tap your head	There is *skull*, a crust on the steel
Touch your backside	The bottom of the ladle has been damaged
Indicate by moving an arm from neck to thigh the shape of a pregnant woman	The converter is full
Run fingers backwards through your hair	Rake off slag
Touch your nose	Put it in the converter's nose
Touch bottom lip or jaw	Refers to the converter's bottom whiskers or its jaws
Touch leg and put up so many fingers	(to crane driver) Pick up a chain with so many *legs*
Tap your shoe	(to crane-driver) Pick up scrap with a fearsome hook called a *shoe*.

The ship-repairing and printing industries are others where the incessant noise demands much sign language; and textiles, e.g. where circling the hands means 'Hurry it up!', is yet another. Choir members in textile towns have been observed mouthing to friends in the congregation. There are cases recorded of originally strong-voiced women having become very softly-spoken by the ends of long careers in the textile industry, whilst their habit of mouthing words has led in ordinary conversation to exaggerated lip movements, especially for *ees* and *oos*, and to lengthened vowels. Always the amount and type of signs depend on working conditions. For example, in heavy electrical engineering, where the crane-driver can see the *slinger* directing his load, they communicate by shouts and ordinary signals, not by other special sign language as in steelmaking. And when conditions change, so does the amount of sign language. Formerly in textiles there was a great deal of lip-reading, e.g. across two looms, because of the incessant rattle (just as now sometimes in car factories). Textile workers did not dare to open windows because this would lower the temperature and because of the poorer easily-broken warp of those days. Moreover, being under threat of instant dismissal if they did anything wrong, they dared not leave their looms. Now, however, with independent ball bearings and electric motors there is less noise, textile workers are readier to take normal tea-breaks, and so they have rather less need for sign language.

Semaphore with lamps or flags and deaf-and-dumb language are special cases for special circumstances. The orthodox version of the last is what the knowledgeable ordinary person can use to a deaf-and-dumb acquaintance (e.g. crossing the second and third fingers of the right hand over the corresponding ones of the left for *f*). It has its uses in emergency. One deaf-and-dumb person lost his wallet on a Lancashire ferry steamer whose skipper, finding it shortly afterwards, raced after him and in the alphabet had reached only *f-o-u* when the passenger embraced him in delight, realising the wallet was found. But amongst themselves deaf-and-dumb people have far quicker methods of communicating such as touching the lips with the right forefinger for 'kiss', holding out the palms for 'book', or, using a sign now in general use, putting up a thumb for 'good'.

The sign language of some occupations is often mentioned, most famous being that of the auction room. Professional bidders are usually very conversant with each other's techniques and fairly open about their bids, having previously decided their limit and never exceeding it. But at certain auctions buyers wanting to avoid a heated and obvious contest with rivals, will arrange with the sales clerk a private code, like partly taking off their glasses or stroking an ear.

Yet there are also industries with a good deal of sign language hardly known about elsewhere. Amongst radio and T.V. technicians, to trace with your forefinger a ring round your ear means 'Not loud enough': to move your hands from the waist apart and then together means 'Stretch it. You are ahead of time'; to touch your neck with your forefinger means 'Cut him off'. Miners too have their signalling codes, such as tapping on a pipe ('I'll knock three if t'deppity's comin' '), or if the mine is noisy, signalling with lamps, tapping on a workmate's shoulder, or pretending to use a spanner, hammer or spade. Lorry drivers may flash their tail lights to warn a following driver that it is dangerous to overtake; or may stick their hand out of the cab window with thumb down as a warning of 'coppers – speed check', or with a vertical circling forefinger meaning 'black ice' (which might send you to heaven).

Sign language is prominent in the leisure industry, the most notable example being that of the tic-tac man on the racecourse or dog-track. Many are the exasperated punters who have tried vainly to decipher his messages in the hope of getting inside information and beating the *bookie*. In cricket there are the umpire's directions for taking guard, his indications of a wide, boundary, six, etc., and his raised finger for 'out'. In Rugby Union the linesman signals which side has to take a line-out and whether a try has been converted. In bowls, by raising three fingers a player tells his partner across the green that three woods are 'in'. The basketball referee, by gradually raising and lowering a finger, signifies 'one point' (from a converted penalty). Two fingers stand for two points (a goal), three for the fact that a player has been in *the zone* round the goal for three seconds, for which a penalty is given, four fingers up would mean that player No. 4 has scored, or clenching both fists that the scorer is No. 10.

But in sport it is the soccer signals that are best known. Think of the referee beckoning a goalkeeper to stop time-wasting, indicating various types of foul and then (vainly) trying to motion the defence away a full legal ten yards, pointing to the dressing-room to send a player off, or to the penalty spot, or half pulling out his notebook in warning. There is the goalkeeper's pointing to an opposing attacker, especially at a corner kick, for the defence to mark him. A frequent contradictory sight is that of a harassed defender clapping to encourage his team when in fact their feeble support is irritating him. Most unexpected of all was Francis Lee's mid-air dive when play was halted at Maine Road, to suggest to the referee and the watching masses that he had been tripped.

It is no surprise that witnesses of sign language who indulge little in it themselves feel rather superior and coin terms for it. To *mee-maw* is grossly to exaggerate the movements of lips and jaw when speaking, a characteristic of

some workers, both male and female. It is generally called
mee-mawin' wi' th' mouth in contrast to flapping the hands
about when speaking, which is *mee-mawin' wi' th' hands*. But
mee-mawing can also stand more generally for being long-
winded; e.g. 'When he'd finished mee-mawin', all he'd said
were . . .'. It is true that some industrial sign language
doesn't have the effect intended. The foreman was explaining
his methods: 'I'm a man of few words, and, when I beckon
you with my finger like this, it means 'Come here like greased
lightning'. The new employee replied, 'I'm a man of few
words myself, and when I shake my head like this it means
'Not bloody likely'. Here for the moment, however, we must
leave this interesting sign-language topic to consider wider
social questions about all forms of industrial language
communication.

Part C Social Context

9 Attitudes to Work and Holidays

Some of us love work and some hate it. A visitor to a small factory was amazed to see a man with his left foot working a pump, with a stick strapped to his right foot stirring a de-greasing mixture, with both hands operating a lathe, whilst reading instructions from a book propped next to it. After hesitating about whether he could spare the time, the man rose hurriedly to shake hands with the visitor, who then saw a curiously squashed grey mixture which he had been sitting on. 'Whatever's that?', he asked. 'Only a bag of putty what I'm pressing to make it work easier.' The other extreme was illustrated where the industrial psychologist noticed that one navvy differed from his mates in always pushing his wheelbarrow upside down. 'Are you sure that is the right way to hold it?', he tactfully inquired. 'Course it is', snarled the navvy. 'If I wheels it right way up, things get put in it.'

Ideally the worker's world is quite a simple one. It is his skill, colleagues, the work setting, getting to and from work, and his family setting; and his language is related to that. He works for *brass, dough, gettings, kelt* or *lolly* and becomes disgruntled if through tax, insurance, lower output etc. it is *bated* (lessened) or if some is *docked*. He may now and then *threeap* (argue), *fratch* or *have a set-to* with his colleagues, but they are part of the comforting regular surroundings. They are his *pals, mates, marrers* (the Geordie word) or *the lads*. *Mates* reminds us how close the ties of work are (cf. *bed-mate* and *soul-mate*); whilst *the lads* (e.g. to officials during a strike, 'I don't know whether that offer'll get the lads back') shows the solid power of union leadership backed, sometimes unwittingly or unwillingly, by rank and file. The book and the film *Saturday Night and Sunday Morning* show particularly well, in ideas at least, attitudes to work and bosses.

Basically, however, the worker is constantly threatened by officialdom and social change, so he lives in his own little world of *the boss, the dole, the sack, getting the push*, or *the boot* or *his cards* (literally through the National Insurance system), whilst others use longer words like *redundancy*. Industrial language for the worker is the reality — *sack* is *sack* and *dole* is *dole*; whereas bureaucratic language like *phased redeployment*, the language of the economic theorist or of the official seeking to hide unpalatable truths, is removed from reality, a sugar-coated pill. Offical language uses such globular and difficult terms. Dr Winstanley's 'This is Your Right' broadcasts are a measure of the complex world in which the worker finds himself, for in these programmes the terms as well as the rights have to be explained. Work language has grown up in a community context, generally in communities rooted in the Industrial Revolution; but is now being replaced, or at least eroded, by a more neutral, official, impersonal language.

The worker resists those who would cut away his homely language as they try to slot him into administrative pigeon-holes. *Social mobility* for him is *having to live in another town, urban development* is *knocking our street down*, and *overspill* is *them bloody chuck-outs* (or *half-castes*) *from Lunnon.*

Fundamentally, society is changing from a tight Victorian-type community to something more bureaucratic and controlled, but there is resistance. Durham County Council in a 1951 report classified their villages into groups A to D, those being allowed to decay being called the D villages, mentioned in the lyrics of the folk singer Alex Glasgow. People do resist change, at least in pockets. People don't want to change. The miners strike for extra *brass* but are quite happy, when that comes, to go on working in miserable conditions down the pit. The continuance of industrial language, fossilised or not, is a measure of people's unwillingness to lose their identity. When workers refer casually to *overspill* etc., John Betjeman's nightmare world of the planner will have arrived.

Industrial language will probably endure because people will always contrive to make new surroundings like the ones they knew. Yet they welcome apparent change where it seems to add to their status. Being *on the line*, working on the production assembly belt in a car factory, with all its din and repetitive actions, is one of the most miserable jobs imaginable, but it becomes slighly more bearable if the unfortunate worker can call himself and be known everywhere as an *assembler*. A wife, asked about her husband in the B.B.C. programme 'Late Night Extra', explained, 'He's a mechanic, but he'd rather be called a motor fitter'. The same tendency is at work in all occupations. This is why every policeman seems to be an *officer*, and why every year a greater and greater proportion of lecturers are *senior* or *principal* ones.

It is said, 'People hate work but like employment'. Often very true: so many of us appreciate the security of employment but not the labour involved. The ideal where work is play and play is work is rarely attained, though some occupations approach it more than others. Contrast the elderly stockbroker, poring over the *Financial Times* at the weekend and clipping out items ostensibly for his files but really for the sheer fun of the thing, with the shift worker on forced overtime to provide a family wage, too exhausted on his days off to do much except potter around.

It is very striking that few words exist for working in an efficient, normal manner. *On the job* is a regular term, and a *one-off job* is a small piece of work turned out quickly and almost incidentally. But, as with the many expressions for foolishness, drunkenness and fighting (see pp. 58–60), it is the unusual that is commented on. So we get for 'working very hard' *fagging, grafting, loustering, riving, slaving, sogging* ('he were sogging away with that file') or *slogging yer guts out*; and *work-brussen*, literally 'work-burst' for 'overdone with work'. Exacting employers are, e.g.., *grinders* or *nigger-drivers* who *hoin* (overwork, harass) their staff. Nevertheless, there are some extraordinary people who are *workish* (fond of work) and eager to *dacker*, i.e. work overtime or spin out work to cause overtime.

The opposite idle attitude seems very prevalent, judging by the many words for it. Governments keep inciting us to work harder like our Continental counterparts, so apparently in Britain there ought to be less *skiving, sliving* or *scrounging*, i.e.

getting out of as much work as possible; *skipping off* or *going for a walk* (e.g. to the toilet) to avoid it; or *shigging*, i.e. throwing up one's job. No one likes to be known as a *great slunting* (idle) *chap*; or a *sleach*, a lazy worthless fellow; or, as they say in Yorkshire, 'so lazy a devil that he can't get up to *laik*' (be off work).

The zeal of many for the end of the working day is shown by the variety of expressions connected with it. First come all the ways of asking the time, e.g. 'What time is it?', 'What time do you call it?', 'Have you got the time on you?', and the curious Durham 'What time have you?', which has puzzled many a stranger. Then, for the time when work finishes for the day, there are *finishing-time, giving-o'er time, lousin'-time*, when the factory *louses* (looses itself), *clocking-out time, knocking-off time, ligging-off time*, etc. On a more serious plane is the saying of one in failing health, 'It's very near six o'clock with him', that being the time, when it was light, when labourers used to knock off work. Also serious are the disturbingly too frequent cases of *sit-down, sit-in*, well-known from the disruptions at Upper Clyde Ship-builders; *work-to-rule, walk-out*, this being an unofficial, often unannounced and spontaneous temporary work stop-page, and the *go-slow*, a deliberate reduction of speed of output equateable with what Scottish miners call the *wee darg* (little day).

Then there are *'ollerdies*. Holiday week, called *Wakes Week* over most of the North, used to be the only period in the year when a major overhaul of many a factory plant could be undertaken. Boiler fires were extinguished, boilers and flues scaled, and all machinery put into good working order. This raises the question, 'Were *wakes weeks* established for the good of the workers or the machinery?'

Local festivals at holiday time still keep their old titles of *club days, fairs, feasts* and *wakes,* and are still prominent in city, town and village; e.g. *Hambledon Club Day, Farningham Fair, Woodhouse Feast* in Leeds, *Owdham* (Oldham) *Wakes*. But the Second World War created big changes in the holiday life of the ordinary man. Up to that there was almost a ritual existence. In Lancashire, for example, holiday weeks were originally fixed in date by industrial leaders, and it seemed that neighbouring towns were never on holiday together, and, when two towns had the same week, one (e.g. Leigh) was occupied with spinning and the other (e.g. Burnley) with weaving. This agreement was obviously intended to ensure that the textile industry did not become disorganised during the holiday season.

Holidays with pay hardly existed before the last war, but now many a works gives a fortnight's holiday and still retains the long weekend at the beginning of September – both holidays with pay. Is the British worker getting *summat* for *nowt*?

During holiday week, inland Northern towns were almost deserted. Ten shillings was often left under the clock to make sure there was enough *brass* left for when the family came back. Main street shops were closed; corner shops in back streets might open for part of the day; even newsagents shut up but usually set up temporary morning news-stands at suitable street junctions and left them in the charge of any man who would take on the job; milk and bread deliveries were restricted, and fresh meat and fish almost unobtainable until food shops reopened on the Thursday and Friday. The shop shut-down is less complete today because the influx of new industry and the decline in demand for other products like coal and textiles have changed the pattern.

In the old-style holiday week, the big town-centre pubs were lifeless but inns in mining areas were well filled because comparatively few miners went on holiday. Part of many a market square or town centre was daily reserved as a parking area for motor-coaches (then called *sharries* or *charrybangs* from *chars-à-banc*) which were assembled there to take on day trips people who had stayed at home. Small shops acted as 'travel agencies' for this minor tourism.

Contrasted with the dreary working weeks the seaside holiday week may have appeared marvellous, but coastal conditions and amenities were often poor. It is alleged that, for one working men's club holiday draw, the first prize was a week in Cleethorpes and the second prize two weeks there. Less believable, except for showing attitudes, was the story that holidaymakers in some resorts, who had been promised reductions if they made their own beds, were then provided with hammer and nails.

On holiday, the social classes were at one time sharply

divided by the food they ate and the places where they ate it.
Workers were happy and comfortable in the type of café
which did not use table linen; had a limited menu of food
that could be warmed up and served with chips; brought
heaped-up platefuls of food direct from kitchen to customer;
provided unlimited bread and butter, several bottles of
sauces, tomato ketchup and vinegar (called in the North
alicker from *ale aigre*); and cups of tea with everything. At one
time, in popular estimation, one could not find a better dish
than fried plaice and chips with 'as much bread and butter as
you can eat'. A *Punch* drawing many years ago accurately
commented on the eating habits of the lower social ranks by
showing the interior of a seaside café and a man saying
angrily to his wife, 'Pass that sauce: this fish tastes of fish'.

Only in extreme circumstances would a pre-war working
man have taken himself into a hotel or good-class restaurant.
He would have been in awe of the aloof male staff; paralysed
by an involved *table d'hôte* and *à la carte* menu and the
armoury of cutlery; would not like to ask for tea (but didn't
like coffee); could think of no other way of attracting a
waiter than whistling or calling *Eigh!*; would not know where
the W.C. was and wouldn't like to ask; would be
conscious of his ill-kept hands and his severely cropped hair;
and would not know how to tip.

Up to 1939, very few people, no matter to what social
station they belonged, had travelled to holiday resorts by air,
and holidays abroad were only for the sophisticates among
the well-to-do. By that day's standards it used to be costly
and the aircraft, which seated about eight people, were
biplanes (all struts and wires). Even in fine weather the flights
were rough and in poor conditions they were frightening.
Weight was critical, and people were turned off flights for
overweighting the crates.

Before the war the working class did little on holiday
except sit on the sands, dance, go to shows and funfairs,
gawp (stare) at shop windows and walk round *Woolies*, and
sit in pubs and cafés; very few went anywhere but the seaside
or possibly London. The walkers who went to the Lake
District, the Yorkshire dales and the Welsh mountains came
normally from the better-educated sections of society,

although church parties did break away from routine to foster hiking· and cycling in quiet parts of the country. Probably the holidaymaker's preference for crowded resorts stemmed from a feeling of security when surrounded by their own folk. Highlights of the holiday would be chance meetings with people from their own town — to meet a neighbour on London Bridge or Brighton Pier would be marvellous. The local press used to recognise this parochialism by printing pictures of holidaymakers with such captions as 'Two happy families who met on the beach at Margate. From left to right . . . . — all from Chelmsford'.

In recent years, holidays have increased and become far more flexible. In many industries like the power industry, workers gladly take odd *looeys*, which, as the name shows, are days off in lieu of a longer holiday period. *Split weeks* have also become fashionable instead of unvarying Saturday-to-Saturday weeks.

Coach-tour holidays in Britain were the means of introducing the working classes to holiday residence in hotels, and after that, thanks to brainwashing publicity, it was not a very formidable step to package holidays in Europe and travel by air. Now there are thousands upon thousands who can take you to Costa Brava cafés where you can get 'a nice cup of tea' and fish and chips, and to bars where English barmen will serve you with English beers — 'just like Blackpool, sarry, but wi' t' sunshine'. Work and holidays have changed beyond all imagination.

10 Slang

Slang in industry shows an attitude to language and thus to society. Slang is the vocabulary used by specific restricted groups (e.g. electricians, nurses, drug-takers or industrial chemists). Unlike dialect it is not confined to particular parts of the country, and so for example *guessing-stick* may be the physicist's slang for his slide-rule no matter where in Britain he was born. Again unlike dialect, slang does not also concern pronunciation, intonation or grammar, but only words. Slang is slung about frequently in industry — perhaps this slinging gives it its name — and the amount of slang there betrays a significantly careless attitude towards the standard language.

Most slang is of recent origin and lasts only a short time. It is generally used by younger people. Older workers use it too but not so readily because, with slang changing so quickly, there is always a danger that, if they use theirs, it will be out of date. Here are some typical passages of recent slang, most of which will soon be past its prime. Can you translate it all?

He'd had a skinful and said 'I'll knock your block off', but shut up when a copper came.

The boxer wore grotty shorts. He was K.O.d in his last punch-up, and turned to booze.

At the next pub were a pile of birds, but most of them were scrubbers so no one tried to pick them up.

I left my mate's pad pretty chuffed after the rave-up last night, but I feel really rough now.

He went messing about on a pub crawl in a shady part of the town, but when someone nicked his buggy while he was puking outside the boozer, and did a bunk and buzzed off with it, he blew his top and went raving bonkers.

Such general slang is nearly always spoken: if written down, it looks so uneducated. Three things seem to give it impetus. First, a search for novelty. Thus, when a sledge-hammer has been called that for so long, it is startling but also refreshing (provided you are not on its receiving end) to hear it becoming temporarily a *persuader*. A second cause of slang is a feeling of gentle superiority, e.g. in calling the man who unloads fish on the docks in the early morning semi-darkness a *lumper* (Fleetwood term), *bobber* (Hull word) or *dock walloper*. A third reason claimed for slang is 'lazyitis', a desire to avoid technical many-syllabled words.

Industrial slang consists largely of old words with new meanings, like *sludge-makers* (steelworkers) or *maintenance wallah*, or else newly invented words like *scuffer* (policeman, presumably because he grabs you by the *scuff*, i.e. scruff, of the neck). Some ideas produce much more slang than others, mainly because they occur so often in conversation. This applies especially to:

1. Parts of the body, most of all the head (*boko, nut, rocker, block, loaf,* etc).
2. Ways of eating and drinking (e.g. *stow it down, swill it*).
3. Methods of speaking (e.g. *claptrap, chunner, blather*).
4. Money (e.g. *brass, dough*).

Besides, the first three do often look comical, and so slang is used to poke irreverent fun at them. Money is a rather different case: here, I think, slang is used to create humour and so hide the embarrassment of the fact that we all think we need it badly and are so eager for it when it comes. Through decimalisation many of the special money names like *bob* and *tanner* have disappeared, and anyone who now goes on saying *I've only a potato pillin'* (shilling) is living in another world. Yet some remain. Recently one drinker, due to pay for the next round, went out to return quickly with something from outside, slapping it onto the bar counter with the remark, 'Here, take it out of that', *that* being a *dustbin lid* (quid).

There is a wide range of slang not generally intended to be offensive. For example, *Get knotted!* is sometimes a reason-ably friendly remark. When speech falls imperceptibly into slang, as it often does, it can cause astonishing remarks, like the reply of the garage proprietor, confronted on a rainy Sunday evening by a motorist whose car had broken down, telling him to *push off*. Then too there are the confusing reasons for entering different occupations — the baker because he *needed* the *dough*, the taxi-driver because he liked bumping into new people, the wallpaperer tired of just hanging about, the biologist because he liked his *grub*, and the sweet-shop owner glad of the *lolly*, the butcher who was always *beefing* about things, and so on.

Strong objections are frequently made against slang, and against surveys of slang, on the grounds that it is silly and trivial. What objectors forget is that slang words are efforts to lighten life and, even if they don't always succeed, the attempt is worth it. The 'good old days' is a misnomer: it was the people who were good, e.g. women who would get up at six to see their menfolk off to work and then stay up past midnight darning those stockings that used to be worn inside clogs. Slang was a welcome relief in those days, as it still is in any tedious occupation.

The industry par excellence for harbouring slang is electrical engineering, since like slang itself that industry is so fast-developing. Headphones are *cans* or *ear-muffs*, a signal generator is a *squeak-box*, oscillating is *squegging*, etc. *More bikes* (cycles) *per sec* is another example, though more of a trainee one.

Slang is also very popular with the industrial chemist and for a similar reason — that growth in his industry is trying to match the pace of civilisation. He talks e.g. of *paddles* (stirrers) or *lollipops* for the four-foot type which comes out with a mass congealed to it, and of *twaddle-sticks* (hydrometers). Unfortunately, besides standing for a measure of degrees of specific gravity, *twaddle* in slang means 'nonsense', and this great contrast in meanings could make an outsider, hearing the chemist refer e.g. to caustic as *70 twaddle per cent*, think he was trying to make a stupid joke.

Less slang is found in the biology laboratory, apart perhaps from referring to a specimen as the *beast* or a scalpel as a knife, which it basically is, and *carving* for dissecting. Other similar phrases sometimes employed are *brew up* or *stew up* meaning to reflux, a process of boiling a mixture without allowing vapour to escape from the container.

Miners, like any other workpeople, enjoy making up words

and will, if they feel like it, call a hammer a *knockometer*, or the plough, a new type of coal-cutter, the *bacon-slicer*. The clothing industry rejoices e.g. in *cabbage* (left-over material); navvies have their *prayer-book* (shovel, because they bow over it) or their *knocker and banjo* (pick and shovel). In the Second World War, destroyers had a *Jack Dusty*, a supply assistant who kept ledgers listing all the stocks, an onerous task usually done at night to the accompaniment of nuts and bolts rolling about in metal racks; and he was aided by an able seaman called a *tanky*. The Merchant Navy weighs in with specialities like *rock-dodger* for coaster, and inland transport comes along with *tubs* for buses and transport café conversations like this:

Doing a flier, are you? (i.e. running up and back in one day, but charging for overnight accommodation).
No, I'm only grabbin' (working overtime), but they've loaded me (i.e. my lorry) so high there's snow on the top.
Are you seeing that skirt (girl-friend) of yours still?
No, she looks awful when she gets the ropes and sheets off.

Slang is not just the prerogative of the male, as hairdressing and nursing terms show. *Bogies* to a hairdresser are not trollies or ghosts or police but head-lice. In the hospitals, a junior nurse is a *sluice-queen*, the container with all necessary equipment for resuscitating a patient is the *crash-wagon*, those elderly men with a common male complaint needing prostatectomy are *bladder daddies*. To give a patient a knee pillow is to *put a donkey in the bed*, whilst to wash and change an infant is to *top and tail it*, which is reminiscent of topping and tailing gooseberries, though naturally we mustn't infer from this that hospital staff of all people believe that babies are found under gooseberry bushes.

Many ways of spending the time which might well be classed by their devotees or victims as part-time occupations are also alive with slang. In ten-pin bowling, where two pins are left, one behind the other, the back one is personified as the *sleeper*; two pins widely separated are a *split*; and odd pins left anywhere are a *washout*. Surfing language, despite

many Americanisms (though the British and Open champion-
ships are held annually in Cornwall), includes plenty of
British slang like *coffin-lid* (surf-board), *baggies* (swimming
trunks reaching to just above the knee), *sleeping* (lying prone
on one's back whilst surfing — much harder than normal
sleeping!); and wave terms like *heavies* (powerful ones
breaking very late near the beach, with consequent danger to
the surf-board), *curlies* (medium-paced and curling at the
tops). and *whites* (wind-affected broken ones providing too
little weight of water for support).

Among less desirable 'occupations' are the worlds of
drug-taking and prison, each full of slang. By *dropping acid*
(injecting a drug) at a *freak-out* (meeting of drug addicts) one
goes on a *trip*. The *pusher* sells drugs and encourages others
to take them, the *junkie* is the drug addict, *shit* is (from its
colour) marihuana or hashish, and so on. In gaol, one's
temporary home is usually the *nick*, a prison officer is a
screw, and tobacco is *snout*. Slang indeed seems all-pervasive.

Sporadically popular is back slang, where words are said
back to front. *Yob* (lout, from *boy* spelt backwards) is at
present well known. The *mho*, the reciprocal of the ohm,
although now an established written technical term, fits
roughly into the same category — please don't make any pun
that it should go home. Most back slang, however, exists only
for a year or two, and within small groups. For instance, in
Manchester a few years ago *lrig*, pronounced *ell-rig*, was a
girl, *talf* was a flat, *drac*, sounded as *dee-rack*, was a card, and
the *Alzap* was the Plaza dance-hall, now renamed the Ritz.
Schoolboys have systems rather similar where every word is
given a suffix, say *-ool*, to make the conversation unintelligible to strangers; but it is precisely because such types of
slang are so hard to follow that they die rapidly, even faster
than normal slang.

Another type is front slang, where each vowel is preceded
by the same invented syllable. Again the purpose has been to
hide the meaning from outsiders, e.g. from the Pakistanis in
textile towns who seem a little isolated because, partly for
more money and partly because established British workers
avoid night work, they get most of the night shifts. A more
important use of this front slang, which prevents it being a

mere fad which completely dies out, is between parents to warn each other and prevent their children hearing — — '*Maig*ind th*aig*at f*aig*ire' for 'Mind that fire'.

Industry is the home of much rhyming slang. It springs from witty working men who want to joke with and surprise their friends. For some reason — perhaps because it is false and therefore touches no tender emotion — women dislike it; but it fascinates children, tickles other men, and makes a curious puzzle for the *Connaught Ranger* (stranger).

What chiefly makes it hard for the visitor to follow is that comparatively straightforward rhyming slang like *tea leaf* (thief) is mixed with shortenings so that the translation has to be made through at least two stages. Thus *titfa* stands for *tit for tat* (hat), *loaf* for *loaf of bread* (head), and 'Where's my Grimsbys?' arises from *Grimsby docks* (socks). Before decimalisation it could be even more complicated; e.g. *Gor a Susy on yer?*, where *Susy* was short for *Susie Anna* = *tanner* = 6d. = 2½ new pence. A second cause of difficulty is that, like ordinary slang, rhyming slang changes fast. Current now, for example, especially round London, is *I'm boracic* from *boracic lint* = *skint* (penniless), a shortening unknown a few years ago. A third obscuring factor is that some of it apparently doesn't even rhyme properly; e.g. *round the houses* (trousers), *I'll have a roast joint* (pint), *bronze figures* (kippers). Still further complications are that occasionally the context is left to show which rhyming slang meaning is intended (e.g. *Irish jigs* can be 'wigs' or 'cigs'); that accepted terms change — *Johnny Randle* (candle) can take another personality in *Harry Handle*; and that often ordinary slang and rhyming slang exist side by side for the same idea (instead of using *Irish jigs* for 'cigs', you can just say *Get me a packet o' coffin nails*).

However, one thing making it more intelligible is that it always seems to have two well-stressed syllables, so drumming home the meaning; e.g. *burnt cinders* (windows), *Mutt 'n Jeff* (deaf), *tea-pot liddin'* (kidding, i.e. teasing), *weeping willow* (pillow) or any of the rhyming slang examples in this chapter. And, if you are irritated by any of the shortened versions, remember that a good reason lies behind them. In ordinary factory language, you wouldn't insult a workmate

by describing in detail something you both know inti-
mately — you wouldn't ask for the *no. 3A flexible sealing
compound* but for the *stuffit* or whatever it is usually
called. Similarly a prisoner just stays in his *flowery*, not
flowery dell (cell), and serves his *bird*, not *bird-lime* (time);
whilst exponents of rhyming slang don't insult each other by
talking about a friend who is *elephant's trunk* (drunk), he's
just *elephants*.

A general belief is that today's rhyming slang is all
Cockney, yet that interesting area has no monopoly over this
particular form of wit. Rhyming slang alters round the
country in both pronunciation and vocabulary. Lancashire's
appas n' purrs equals Cockney *apples n' pears* (stairs); and
other terms like *Wheer's mi Whalley Range* (change) or
Wheer's mi Newton Heaths (teeths - an odd double plural)
depend on knowing districts of Manchester. The last term, in
fact, equals London's *'Ampstead 'Eath*, often shortened to
'Ampsteads, and would be little use outside the metropolis. It
also varies with occupation, bricklayer's type being amongst
the most unintelligible. An example of this would be: 'Now, my
china plate (mate), no more laugh an' a joke (smoke), out
with yer cherry ripe (pipe), off with yer steam packet
(jacket) and let's have some Russian Turk (work). Get yer
bark n' growl (trowel) on to them Dublin tricks (bricks).
Where's the Lord Lovel (shovel)? Now bring me some
fisherman's daughter (water).'

Much rhyming slang comes from the names of people,
usually of a bygone age. Thus *Duke of York* (table fork),
Aunt Maria (fire), *Baden Powell* (towel), *Boo Peep* (sleep),
Jack the Rippers (slippers). From the old boxer's names
come *Jem Mace* (face) and *Jimmy Wilde* (glass of mild), from
old entertainers *Mickey Roon* (spoon, with the surname's *-ey*
lost) and *Wilkie Bards* (cards).

Most rhyming slang concerns important things like food,
drink and money. A *Jimmy Skinner* (dinner), starting with
loop the loop (soup), might include *jockey's whips* (chips),
stand at ease (cheese) and a *cup of you an' me* (tea). But
when anyone's *currant bread*, this has nothing to do with
food, or at least he's right off it, for in fact he's dead.

In the pub you can ask for a pint of *pig's ear* (beer), a

Charlie Frisky (whisky) or a *Tom Thumb* (rum) before you go out on the *frog and toad* (road). If there's no *rock of ages* (wages), there may well be a *bull an' cow* (row) with your *trouble an' strife* (wife). But, if you're on the *cob an' coal* (dole), though you will be unpopular at the *cab rank* (bank), you'll draw plenty of *bees an' honey* (money) if you have, say, five *God forbids* (kids).

Other essentials like clothing and parts of the body need names. Thus, if you are going to the *dolly mixtures* (pictures), you might first have a *dig in the grave* (shave) with some *Band of Hope* (soap) before putting on a new *dicky dirt* (shirt) and a *whistle an' flute* (suit). If you suffer an accident whilst having a *stick of chalk* (walk), you might yell *Oh, mi mince pie!* (eye) or *What's broken mi Lancashire lasses?* (glasses). Or, depending on where you are hurt, *Ow! mi lump of lead!* (head) or *I suppose* (nose) or *north an' south* (mouth), or *bird's nest* (chest) or *hammer an' tack* (back) or *German band* (hand) or *comic singers* (fingers) or *chips an' peas* (knees) or *plates of meat* (feet).

Finally, since bingo has become so much an occupation, especially for the ladies, it would be appropriate to list some of their rhyming terms, namely:

1. buttered scone
2. me an' you
3. you an' me (or *up a tree*)
4. knock at the door
5. all alive
6. Tom Mix (or, more modern, *chopping sticks*)
7. God's in heaven
8. Harry Tate
9. Hospital (No rhyme: from No. 9 pills formerly given in the Army)
10. Cock an' hen
11. legs eleven
12. monkey's cousin (dozen)

Plus other concoctions like *clickety-click* (66); and *cannock-nuff* (49), from the Great War attempts at the French *quarante-neuf*.

With so much general and specialised slang trying to take hold of ordinary spoken language, it can be criticised or enjoyed, but never ignored.

11 Uncouth Language

Most industries are a man's world, and this is given as the reason for the allegedly rough and uncouth language that is often so deep-rooted there. When gentle, feminine-sounding words are heard, their very unusualness makes them stand out. A striking case is in fishing language, where the word for making a net is often *makkin', mekkin'* or *braidin'*, all good solid masculine-looking terms, but where over great stretches of the British coastline the men say they *knit* them. In Wales the equivalent is *gwau* (to weave, to knit). Language-wise these fishing ideas seem inconsistent, but no more so than the fisherfolk's actions at Newbiggin, Northumberland, where till recently, and before the days of 'Women's Lib.', the women had the masculine task of hauling the cobles up the beach.

In Chapter 1 we noted word-parts appealing to or connected with the fair sex, like *-ette* (*epaulette, majorette*), *mini-* (mini-skirt, mini-book), and *-y* or *-ie* (*hanky, nightie*). *Clippie*, for example, sounds an appropriately feminine name for a bus-conductress, though a conductor might well resent it. Where a man puts up with this type of name, like the *clocky* who clocks people in and out of a factory, he does so comforted that he is being referred to in a slangy joking way without reflection on his masculinity.

But with rare exceptions, like those just mentioned, industrial language can appear quite often raw, vulgar and starkly masculine. It can range from the exasperated *You silly git!* of the cyclist leaving the factory and finding on a roundabout an impatient motorist dangerously crossing his bows, to the most undictionary-like, outwardly offensive and embarrassing language possible. Straight away the casual visitor to a building site, mine, docks or other workplace should be warned especially about the amount of swearing, for some workmen could not swear more if they tried.

Whether swearing is on the increase is a moot point. The student from a sheltered home taking his first vacation job in a factory is surprised by it and nearly always thinks it must

be increasing. Older hands will agree. Generally, they say, in
the olden days it burst out only when a man met a snag,
whereas now it is common in normal conversation. Whether
this true or whether it is part of the halo an old-timer
unconsciously erects around his past, believing that everything was better in the olden days, is hard to say. Certainly it
was always prevalent (for a literary angle compare George
Orwell's *Down and Out . . .*), and a great deal of it is used
today. As for the future, it cannot easily get much worse but
is unlikely to get significantly better.

There is much social pressure to swear. Some workmen
swear more to show their superiority over newcomers. If you
don't join in, you are thought an outsider, or at least
eccentric, so gradually unless your previous upbringing proves
very strong you swear like the rest. It has even been claimed
that swearing is unexpectedly increasing in offices, shops and
among white-collar workers where dealing with the general
public should be a powerful restraining and mellowing factor.
When someone from a 'politer' occupation says something
meaty, eyebrows are raised — taking another literary example,
compare the monk in Pinter's *Car :taker* who says *piss off!*

Most commentators would agree that the presence of
women, e.g. in pub and club, cuts down the swearing — even
miners fresh from the pit will swear less there because there
are women around — but they maintain that swearing increases in proportion as respect for women decreases through
women's partly successful fight towards 'equality of the
sexes'. However, in a prolonged strike many workers miss the
lack of verbal restraints that makes life in industry bearable,
for uncouth language is not suitable in the home.

Chanted swearing at football matches shows that swearing
is on the increase there. Previously individual spectators
swore at their fallen favourites or at particularly brutal
opposing players, but there was no collective swearing. The
new type has no great meaning. It is like the football crowd's
mindless baying of 'You'll Never Walk Alone', which one is
tempted to think, signifies little more than that home team
supporters will band together to fight visiting fans or, when
released from the ground, to create acts of disappointed
hooliganism against nearby shops. Swearing also seems to

have increased in grammar schools. Do teachers notice this, and is it because selective schools are taking a wider spread of the population? Little boys in long trousers on trains now swear, and the language is thought to be increasing with women and schoolgirls in urban areas.

Does growing education cut down swearing? It obviously increases vocabulary and arguably is supposed to improve character, and for both reasons one might think that there would be less swearing. Yet, although education may curtail it, it can never stop it. The educated postgraduate chemist, if something goes wrong — if, say, someone accidentally spills concentrated acid over his results — will break out into violent language or, even if he seems so impeccable as to maintain outward calm, will be saying something fierce to himself.

Still, it is to be hoped that education is some counter-influence. Apart from any moral issue, it would be sad in these days of widening mass education if swearing were on the increase, for its vocabulary is so limited. Just as *nice, nasty, awful,* etc., lose most of their meanings through over-use, so do swear words. It is strange that industry, so rich in technical nouns, should be very restricted in adjectives, and hopelessly so if most of them are swear adjectives. This is not preaching but plain linguistic fact.

In British factories, the link between formal religion and absence of swearing may be very weak, if present at all. Other considerations are greater, like the amount and type of parental influence. Thus teenagers in Pakistan and Saudi Arabia for example are not allowed to swear in the presence of their fathers because of the much stricter parental control there, where the father is the only breadwinner and would cut down or cut off his assistance if necessary. In Britain we find slacker discipline and, partly because of this and the sanction of television, etc., more swearing.

There may be some truth in the assertion that British swearing is more blasphemous than that of other countries, e.g. France and Spain, because they are more religious than ours. On the other hand, religious Irish workers seem to swear a good deal. Blasphemous swearing, like the ordinary type, comes from trying to strengthen a remark. It used to be deliberately shocking, blasphemy in our grandparents' time being one of the vilest sins. Today, however, such British swearing has lost its blasphemy. *God* in swearing has almost lost its religious connections, and *bloody*, when thought about at all, is linked with *blood* rather than its true religious origin *By our Lady!* Often part of the expression is euphemistically clipped or omitted — *Zounds!* from *By God's wounds!*; *Oh my!*; or just *By!*, a favourite in the North-East. Alternatively it is distorted or disguised; e.g. *bloody* to *bloomin'* or *blinkin'*, *damnation* to *tarnation*, *damn* to *dash* or *darn*, *hell* to *heck(y)*, *God* to *gosh, golly* or *gock*.

Bloody is still the commonest adjective among all swearing age-groups, that and *flaming* being favourites among older people. Where an apparently objectionable object can be seen, it is normally given, not its real name, but a stock adjective, so that a miner, warning his mate about a prop, would just say *Mind that bloody thing!*

Leaders of industry, from heads of the great nationalised concerns down to the lowliest chargehand, can be subject to frequent abuse, triggered off by the impact of authority rather than anything personal. Thus the pit-head foreman can be in polite language *boss*, in County Durham *keeker* (because he *keeks* or spies on lazy workers), or *gaffer*; but also is often sworn at or referred to by various uncomplimentary titles to be investigated shortly. In road transport, the loader who fills a vehicle so badly that a driver has to make nineteen or twenty *drops* instead of a few, receives an alarming set of swear names and angry descriptions.

Swearing is curious. People often object to it on T.V., in plays which are only fictitious, and yet swear like troopers at work. Is this because they unconsciously fear that their children will fall into the same habits, which may restrict their social and employment opportunities? The ultimate, of course, is the not unusual practice of inserting a swearword in the middle of an ordinary one. To sum up, swearing is basically for one of two reasons. It is either a gesture of independence against authority, as with the schoolboy; or else it is ritualistic, as e.g. with market porters and hardened building workers, where it is integrated with the rest of their language.

Apparently vulgar language is not always to shock. For

someone falling head over heels, besides variants like *bully-necks over* and *back'ards way over*, we find *arse over tit*, but only as the clearest way a workman can express the incident. In the days when poverty forced mothers to cut down older children's clothes for younger members of the family, no attempt would be made to ensure a fit, and small boys were compelled to wear trousers several sizes too big for them. Of such unfortunates, the head of the house would say, *He favvers* (seems to be) *all arse an' pockets*. The same applied to employees whose clothing was bought by their wives and mothers at market stalls and jumble sales. Again, these are just appropriate descriptions. Steelworks use flexible 1½″-diameter hoses for connection to the electric-arc furnaces. Their metal ends, which may be pinched together to get a longer flame of gas or jet of water, are vividly called *pissers*. Orders for them inside the works are not written out: the men go themselves to collect them from stores. How typists at headquarters indent for them is a different matter.

When the fisherman talks of the *arse-end* of a net or the wind from right behind his boat blowing *up yer arse* or when the farmer mentions the *arse-board* of his cart, they are using, not only good old Anglo-Saxon words, but technical terms. The cow not giving full milk because it is *blind o' one pap* or *deaf o' one tit*, is a similar technical description, as are farmers' terms for a cow's vagina. One child, on holiday at her aunt's country farm, was warned, 'Mind them turds'. Later at her grandmother's farm, where the pigs had been equally messy, she was told, 'Mind them tooards'. Surprised, she said her aunt didn't call them that, to which her grandmother replied, 'Oh her! She awlus did talk polite'.

Sexual language in industry is rather parallel to swearing in that much of its original meaning has gone. Otherwise presumably, as their sexual desires wane, we should find it markedly decreasing amongst those elderly speakers who in the fire of their youth and the tenacity of their middle age have been very fond of the words. In Victorian times it was though the height of wickedness and absolutely taboo to mention sex, and therefore by perverse reaction sex words have been brought into conversations deliberately. But now they mean far less. When someone in industry says 'I'm gonna fuck 'im', 'I got fucked for this' or 'I got ballocked left, right and centre', it refers only to a reprimand. This disappearance of sexual meanings is no new thing. Before the last war a Lancashire miner who during his kitchen bath had been surprised by a visitor, might say on recounting the incident, 'An' theer Ah wur — stark ballock-naked', not conscious that he was referring to his genitals. Similarly the boss may be called *yon silly owd bugger, that right twat* or *that bastard* quite unconnected with his supposed personal behaviour, sex or illegitimacy.

Now, with Great Britain's entry into the Common Market, when the literal translations of words or phrases do not always carry the same meaning in one language as in another, the problems posed would be enormous. An excellent example is in metalwork, where the standard textbook name for the second roughest file is *bastard*. Now obviously, if it is translated by an interpreter who does not understand the industrial terms, to say that confusion can arise is an understatement.

Many directly sexual terms are in vogue, like *queer (fellow)* or the Merchant Navy term *golden rivet* for a homosexual. An infuriated spectator may shout at a plump, sleek referee, 'You nasty little ponce!' (or *puff*); and, if a nearby fan argues, say to him 'You cheeky sod!' or 'Sod off, will you?', still probably continuing the sexual language. Some terms however, in spreading from technical language to popular speech, have almost lost their erotic element. A *sadist* is usually just cruel or callous, and a *masochist* just someone who, for example, seems to enjoy continual work. Other terms are almost unrecognisable because the sexual fuse seems to have gone out of them. Possibly relevant here are *he's soft, stuck up, they can't get on together, he's hard, up n' coming, a big shot*, and especially *come to a sticky end*. Yet the origins of these last examples are a matter of conjecture, and there is a danger of overemphasising the supposed sexual element. If, for instance, you were to see young miners *mauling about i' t'raw* and hear them conversing in the pit-head baths, you might form the impression that they were a lot of homosexuals, though nothing could be farther from the truth.

Still, there is no denying that from time to time direct
sexual overtones do come in. *Fettle*, besides being a
well-known steel and engineering industry word for 'mend',
often means to achieve sexual intercourse. A question asked
of a youth who has been out with a girl is, 'Well, did you
fettle 'er?' *Plump in fettle* means exuberantly healthy,
attractive and ready for anything. A man admiring a lively
shapely girl may say, 'By God, she's plump in fettle'. This
plump, by the way, could perhaps be a mispronunciation of
plumb from building language, since *plumb right* and *plumb
on* mean 'exactly'. *Mauling about* means 'associating with'
and what follows, e.g. 'He's been mauling about with that big
lass out o' Norris Street'. Of an impatient lover, *e's awlus in a
'urry* and *awlus at t'last shove-up* are used sexually and quite
respectfully. *It's a poor game to be good at*, besides referring
e.g. to drinking to excess or cheating at gambling games,
often concerns someone who has been doing too much
womanising, especially with a married woman. Finally there
is the expression *that there*. Long before the song 'You can't
do that there here', Northerners used *that there* as a
euphemism for the sexual act. It is a standard phrase in the
north when youngsters of both sexes are 'educating' themselves by discussing sex matters; and for adults who don't like
to use one of the obscenities but don't know the more polite
words.

Such words are so deeply ingrained in some men's
vocabulary that they just can't understand the equivalents
from other layers of speech. Striking instances keep occurring
in hospital wards, especially among elderly patients. A nurse
will ask, 'Have you had your bowels moved?' and, when
greeted by a blank stare or irrelevant answer, will have to
translate, 'No, I mean "Have you had a shit?"' To take
another example, normally patients sign an agreement to 'an
operation or operations', but for a certain one *testicles* is put
on the form of agreement. Many workmen seem quite
ignorant of this word and their nurse has to give the latest
slang for it.

However, compilers of modern dictionaries may be going
too far. All words, including swearing and sexual ones, are
best met in a living context, not enshrined in a dictionary. It

is thought that most etymologists have on occasion eagerly sought meanings and quotations concerning the various erotic words in the larger dictionaries, but whether the claim is true is most doubtful. It does not seem a greatly exciting hobby, and the interest might be better served e.g. by scrutinising certain of the very popular magazines. But without doubt some dictionaries do contain a startling array of sexual words. In Partridge's *Dictionary of Slang and Unconventional English*, one feels that the second element has achieved undue prominence in comparison with his treatment of slang, yet even he guardedly set down the two most famous four-letter words as *f*ck* and *c**t*, whereas the latest (1972) supplement to *The Oxford English Dictionary* has abandoned all restraint and given them the full treatment. This new permissiveness is in many respects overdone. As a thoughtful article in *New Society** points out, taboo words are fascinating just because they are taboo: the taboo is part of the meaning.

Dictionaries, by their detailed consideration of sexual words, can actually pull in a different direction from that intended by living language. Although most workmen feel free to express themselves as they wish to their pals and work-mates, many fear that such choice language will spurt out from them at home and try to suppress it there. When they become family men, some of them moderate their language quite a lot, e.g. the average married garage mechanic is far more restrained in his language than the typical unmarried *brickie*. A few less inhibited and usually elderly workers express surprise at the decay of four-letter words well entrenched in their own vocabulary, pointing to the efficiency of those words in sounding like what they represented. Of course they are wide of the mark, for sexual terms usually decay, not through any wrong decision about their structural merits, but by the attack of euphemisms.

Toilets and associated matters are prime examples of unorthodox language. Although many euphemisms for them (noted in Chapter 14) are current, a word count would show that in industrial language the uncouth alternatives are much

*19 October 1972, p. 156.

commoner. At home, when reminding his children of such bodily functions, the worker restrains himself, e.g. uses *trumped* (like a trumpet) for the more vulgar *farted*; *pee, wickle* or *piddle* for to urinate; *lav(vy)* for the toilet; or *'Ave you bob-bawed?* for 'Have you emptied your bowels?'. And occasionally amongst workers, men or women, of the same sex a surprising bit of philosophy may overlie the rougher meaning. *Clean face, dirty knickers*, for example, is a waspish comment on the type of woman who arrives home from work about 6 p.m. and at a quarter past goes out for the evening all dolled-up.

At work, however, things are different. Outstanding in this perhaps quixotic language corner is the marked class difference shown in making selections. The boss or executive may state 'I'm just going to wash my hands', though they are quite clean, or 'I'm off to pump ship', or – using a middle-of-the-road term – 'I'm just nipping down for a pee' (euphemism for *piss*); whereas at very labouring level the expressions appear much coarser. In a large factory, the odd-job-man or *dogsbody* may be told, 'We're out of bloody bog-roll. Get some'; and almost every minute some worker there is mentioning *piss, the bogs, shit-house*, etc. To 'Where's Bert?', the correct answer may be, 'He's gone for a quiet crap' or 'He's gone for a crafty shit'. So here lies another unorthodox language element that in all fairness has to be investigated. Indeed, if we were to conclude that much shop-floor language is grounded on the vulgar, obscene or uncouth, we shouldn't be far wrong.

Part D Can it be Understood?

12 Simplification

After all the curious terms so far dealt with, the burning question is 'How far can occupational language be generally understood?' Well, the average Britisher can follow it much better than German with its different spelling, inflexions and word order, or French with its foreign vocabulary , or pidgin English with its baby grammar and wording. Whilst the man-in-the-British-street may be puzzled by *Seekrank* or *mal-de-mer* or *belly-belong-me-walk-about-too-much*, he should understand *the bellyache* or *t'belly-warch*.

Industry has a tendency to shorten technical words and give them more homely names. Double-barrelled names are often reduced to their first words, so that a *brickie* (bricklayer) calls a bulldozer a *dozer* and a claw-hammer a *claw*. In distillation, whatever comes out first and last are *tops and tails* or *tops and bottoms*; in nursing, the peculiarly spelt and said oesophagus becomes just the *food channel*; in factories, *Where does he live?* means 'Where is his office?' and *stop fortnight* is the works holiday period. In railway shunting, the *hump* is an embankment in reception sidings, and waggons are *cut*, not unhooked; musicians talk about *reading dots* for sight-reading music; whilst at sea the anchor is often the *hook* and the telescope a *spy-glass*, and in the Merchant Navy masts are *sticks*, though this flippant term would make many an old sea-dog turn in his grave. *Sticks* to the linesman and electrician are telegraph poles (He has to *shin up the stick*), and the *block* is a big power station.

People are also referred to in a familiar way, ignoring their titles. A well-known county education officer, famous and respected both in and out of teaching, was known to most of his teachers as *Jack*, though etiquette forbade their saying it to his face. In factories, 'Father's coming down today' may refer to the manager, *Uncle Les* to the foreman, and *Ma* to the tea-woman. And don't forget *Brother*, with its family and political implications . . . .

Another very common method of simplifying is to

101

abbreviate by using what is really a professional shorthand in speech. Failure to use it may be taken as an insult. If the foreman were to say, 'Let's have a no. 5A rolled steel bar now', the workman might respond, 'What's up with yer? Think I don't know mi bleedin' job? Think I don't know what an Irish B is?'

Abbreviation is effected in four ways: by reducing expressions to their starts, starts and ends (with middles lost), ends only, or just initials. Where only the starts are left, they include such well-known ones as *lab* (laboratory), *subs* for substitutes or subscriptions, *refs* (references), *reps* (representatives — a newer term for commercial travellers), *gym*(nasium) and *demo*(nstration). Another is *caf*, cafeteria. Many are less widely known but quite common within the industries concerned. Thus, contrasting with some ungainly conglomerations like *decompression ratio*, mechanical engineering wisely has available *thou* (1/1000 inch), *carb* (carburettor) and *sparker* (sparking-plug). Similarly, to save repeating the full term, road transport has the *artic* (articulated vehicle); battery-making firms have the *pos* and the *neg*; steelmaking has *grans* (granite chippings) and to mend the furnace *dally* (dalofrit); and biology uses *streps* (streptococci), *prots* (protozoa) *and bacti* for the bacteriology laboratory. Nursing knows the friendly, almost human *Auntie Flo* for an antiphlogistine poultice, and the euphemistic *mag sulf* for magnesium sulphate or Epsom salts.

Some of these are graphic shortenings, from seeing the abbreviated word in print — *gent* (gentleman), *sov* (sovereign), *ad* (advertisement). In others, the later part of the expression is understood, as in 'We used to come from Gloucester with the slow' (i.e. slow train), or the slogan infamous for endangering children's spelling, *Drinka pinta*, where milk is understood.

Expressions which have lost their middles provide the next group: *motel* from motor + hotel and *botel* (boat + hotel); *breathalyser* (no explanation surely needed); *trafficator* (traffic indicator), *espiscope (epidiascope), rotovator* (rotary cultivator), *frood* (frozen food), The *doffer* in a textile mill does the *doffing* from *do off* or taking off the full bobbins before replacing them with empty ones. Another example with head and tail but no body is *gunk* for both a re-solvent and surplus equipment, which seems delightfully named from government + junk.

Sometimes, especially in electronics, these terms even after losing their middles remain highly technical — *immittance*, a generic word covering impedance and admittance; *shiftrix* (shifting matrix);*indusistor* (inductive transistor). Fortunately the trade itself sometimes recognises the meaning barrier to these words, as indicated in this advertisement in *Electronics Weekly:** 'And what the . . . [space here for you to supply a suitably strong noun] is a FRITCH? A frequent twitch? Or a frozen pitch maybe? Actually, it's a *frequency-responsive switch*', after which you are urged to 'send to day for our full FRITCH switch pitch' (i.e. range). Even more general words of the lost-middle type don't always seem short enough — e.g. *foodtainer* for a light plastic food container. Would the average worker, calling at his *chippy* or *fish-oil* (fish-and-chip shop), really want to ask for 'fish n' chips twice in a foodtainer'? It seems unreal.

Although some of the lost-middle shortenings are too timid, others because of their simplicity strike popular imagination, like *Chunnel* for the projected Channel Tunnel. Unfortunately there goes with the last example an idea that *chunnel* workers will be just as simple. The story is related of the Irishman who submitted for it the ridiculously low tender of £22,222-22p., stating that he and his three sons would excavate it, working with pick and shovel only, two from each side. When the architects asked, 'Are you sure you can? What if the two tunnels don't meet?', Paddy replied, 'Bejabers, that's all right. Then you'd get two for the price of one'.

Where only the ends of expressions are left, they can be normal abbreviations like *bus* or *phone*; or cases where the first word is omitted because any fool is supposed capable of mentally adding it. To the lorry driver the *lights* are not Blackpool Illuminations, nor the *island* a desert one with dusky swaying maidens; and to a Fylde railwayman 'He lives near North' can refer only to the station, Blackpool North.

*11 October 1972.

Many other end-abbreviations, like *prentice* for apprentice, are caused by dropping a first unstressed syllable. Fishing has the *lectric ray*, and the *creasing* for increasing, i.e. widening, the row of meshes in a net. There are, of course, many others — *cos, lastic, leven, lotments, tice, sizes* (assizes), *baccy, tayter* as in *tayter-pie*, and so on. And do we realise that we are slaughtering words every time we use the important conversational aids *scuse me* ('Excuse me') and *Kyoo* ('Thank you')?

About the most extreme form of abbreviation is the use of initials. Its very shortness makes it so easy to use, and is one reason why unions and the like are well-known to the general public. Think, for example, of the N.U.R., A.S.L.E.F., A.E.U., N.U.T., B.A.L.P.A., the C.B.I., the T.U.C., and so on. Although the broadcaster forecasts temperatures in *Centigrade*, among scientists terms like *700 degrees C* are the norm. In the various trades and occupations, many other examples appear. The physicist uses *g* for gravitational, the Army A.B.M. for anti-ballistic missile; and on the platform of places like Liverpool St Station, which have no separate parcels depot, you can always see BRUTES, which are the cages nicknamed from British Rail Universal Trolley Equipment. As technical change accelerates, miners for instance use more and more abbreviations, like *Harvey R.V.*, and especially for electrical switchgear, like *T.B.60* and *S.M.2*, respectively types of conveyor-belt drive and switch-unit control. These are generally trade names and are used in parrot-like fashion.

In hairdressing, a few years ago one style was known by the ladies who wore it as the *D.A.*, politely 'duck's anatomy' or more indelicately 'duck's arse', since that is what it resembled. Hairdressing schools teach the need to approach the client with the *three Cs*, namely comfort, cover and comb. Nursing, another occupation dominated by the fair sex, is also very fond of initials, not only for rapid speech — *P.P.* (private patient), *G.P.* (general practitioner), *O.B.E.* (oil, bath and enema); but sometimes to hide an unpleasant meaning, like *C.V.A.* (cerebro-vascular accident), *B.P.* (blood pressure), *B.(N.)O.* (bowels (not) open), or *D.O.A.* (dead on arrival). An incident recently reported is of a new nurse, told to see to a case of *B.I.D.* Thinking it was just another disease she did not fully understand, innocently she approached the stretcher, to be horrified on seeing that, as the abbreviation tells, the man had been brought in dead. Her consternation was understandable because initial abbreviations in nursing stand for all sorts of things. Care has to be exercised, as they are seen or heard by patients as well as medical and nursing staff. Alliteration, slang and a desire to hide the meaning all contribute to the *three Hs*, standing for 'high, hot, and a hell of a lot', and used when a soft soap and water enema has to be applied. Where illnesses are undetermined, patients tend to be impressed by splendid abbreviations like *P.U.O.* (pyorrhoea of unknown origin), *N.Y.D.* (not yet diagnosed), *N.A.C.* (not a clue) and *G.O.K.* (God only knows!).

Admittedly, for the countless abbreviations there are only the twenty-six letters of our alphabet, which in theory could make for ambiguity; but context usually prevents it. A patient receiving the *O.B.E.* above is not going to a Buckingham Palace investiture; a nurse mentioning *B.P.* is unlikely to be considering her shares in British Petroleum; and the engineer calculating in *thous* (thousandths of an inch) will be thinking differently from the trawler skipper, to whom a *thou* is a beautiful thing, £1000.

A rare refinement is to reverse an abbreviation. A *codon* in biology is a sequence of three nitrogenous bases found on a gene in a certain molecule. Conversely, there is a trio of bases which signify the end of a gene. Previously in Britain they were known as *anti-codons*, but now because of American influence people are beginning to call them *nodocs*, from *codon* spelt backwards. The shortest abbreviations of all, relying on one initial only, are found chiefly in the international Q code, which enables a radio operator to carry on sensible conversations with colleagues anywhere in the world.

Doubtless the industry fondest of abbreviations is electrical engineering, and its massive proportion of abbreviated new words is still growing.* At times it amounts to an

---

*According to my analysis of various glossaries of E. M. Codlin, A. K. M. Green, and C. K. Moore, it was in 1963 27.7 percent, in 1966 31.4 percent, and in 1969 no less than 38.8 percent or approaching half.

obsession. Consider e.g. the short and comprehensible *mini-track* for a satellite tracking and data acquisition network, which from its initials has been changed to the less obvious *stadan.** Perhaps the best-known electrical abbreviation, because premium bondholders are so incurably optimistic, is *Ernie* (electronic random number indicator equipment). Many of these electrical abbreviations by initials are easy to remember. They can be geographical, like *safari* for semi-automatic failure anticipation recording instrumentation (try saying that mouthful to a helpess listener!), or *Asia* (automatic sensitivity indicator alarm). Another group are the culinary ones, like *donut* (digitally operated network using thresholds), although the layman would need both a strong head and a strong stomach to digest them.

However, the largest and most interesting group of electronic abbreviations is for people made alive. Of this kind are *Ernie*, already mentioned, *Vera* for 'vision electronic recording apparatus' developed by the B.B.C., and *Elvis* (compare the 'pop' singer Elvis Presley) for 'electro-luminescent vertical integrating system'. Their coining is made easier by including or omitting initials of unimportant words as desired, e.g. in *dame* (data acquisition [and] monitoring equipment), *Isabel* (iso status accumulating binaries [using] extraordinary logic). Alternatively more than a word's first letter may be taken, e.g. *Maude* (*mo*rse *au*tomatic *de*coding). If you feel here that coiners of words are bending the rules to suit their own convenience, do be lenient with them, for they are trying to simplify what linguistically is a very difficult industry. They will have to bear much hostile criticism anyway. Look, for instance, at *bmews* for 'ballistic missile early warning system — an abbreviation hard to say and enough to bemuse any speaker!

Molecular biology is a very complex subject and the molecules themselves are relatively very large and complex. Their names are often long and even if pronounceable create difficulties with spelling. To abbreviate them, as does the chemistry, to molecular formulae is a more arduous task than naming them by a simple abbreviation. Thus deoxyribose

**Interavia*, 19, no. 3 (March 1964) 292.

nucleic acid, ribosenucleic acid and adenosine tri-phosphate become respectively *D.N.A., R.N.A.,* and A.T.P., shortening up to ten syllables down to three. Their meanings are widely understood amongst biologists and biochemists.

Again, in physics letters and symbols are used to represent words, such as μ meaning the permittivity of a substance or β meaning magnetic flux density. You may think that *Bev* is a shortened form of a proper name, but in fact it is an expression for the force action on an electron of a magnetic field.

Let us consider symbols for a moment in more detail. In mathematics, symbols replace words and letters represent unknown quantities. E.g. the statement '$3x + 2 = y$' means that three of the quantities which for convenience are denoted by x added to two units are equal in size to another quantity denoted by y. Another example of a relatively short phrase meaning a great deal is as follows:

$$\begin{matrix} p \\ \int \\ q \end{matrix} /\xi x: \frac{dy}{dx} \; 3x^2 - x = 0/\Leftrightarrow x\epsilon \; \{\text{real nos} \; \forall \; x \geqslant 7\}$$

Translation: the integral between the limits of p and q of the modulus of the algebraic sum of x, such that the differential of the expression $3x^2 - x = 0$, implies that x is any element of the set of real numbers for all values of x which are greater than or equal to 7.

Mind you, beware of referring to a *number* because you may possibly be talking about integers, natural numbers, real numbers, rational numbers or complex numbers. You must also distinguish between positive and negative, taking note of zero.

Symbols are often used in scientific papers. One of the most common in biology is $\female$ for female and $\male$ for male. They are like shorthand forms. In chemistry, you come across symbols like pH, pKa and pKb, which have no literal meaning but are expressions of the acidity or basicity of a compound. To outsiders, $NOT_e \; B_e N_e$ could be easily mistaken for the Latin term meaning 'note well', but to a chemist it denotes a mixture of the elements nitrogen, oxygen, helluvium, beryllium and neon. In chemistry, the symbol ⬡ means benzene, which has a long chemical formula. Using this type of notation, a chemical formula which would look complicated and confusing written out fully, will appear relatively simple and easy to follow.

Various qualifications are, however, needed about the worth of industrial abbreviations. Motorists will have realised long ago that, say, the M61 is not the sixty-first motorway built, merely one connected with the M6, but many abbreviations need more care. Firstly, like any other words they can fall suddenly out of favour — e.g. *mals*, the old shortening for members of an amalgamated society, is uncommon now. Secondly, some are alien to certain industries — e.g. *temp* (temperature), used on many a shop floor, is outside the language of the industrial chemist. Thirdly, in some areas of industry like chemistry, most abbreviations are written and few said. Next some, like eq^b or eq^1 for equilibrium, eq^n for equation and $\downarrow$ for precipitation, can never be said at all. Finally, although it is commonly imagined that abbreviations like *P.N.T.* or *M.E.K.* are highly efficient time-savers, they can actually hinder efficiency, e.g. in some branches of industrial chemistry, where the trainee has to spend so long attempting desperately to understand them all. Abbreviations are no cure for every industrial-language headache.

Industry's clear, vivid comparisons do help meaning a great deal. It is true that its language also teems with fossilised metaphors — *coats of paint, clock-face, shoe-tree, will it wash?, get it taped, works branch*. But most metaphors that have sprung from one industry into general use are expressive and vigorous — from poultry farming comes a *bad egg*, from the clothing industry *tailor-made*, from brewing *all grist to the mill*. From electronics comes a description of a theatre performance as *electrifying*, or of a man as a *live wire* — and he becomes an extended metaphor when a cynic grumbles that he would be dead but for his connections.

Other comparisons which aid understanding include cases of the thing meant being represented by something closely linked with it (called metonymy), as with: the turf (horse-racing), the press (newspapers), Throgmorton Street (the British stock market), Harley Street, Wardour Street and Carnaby Street (respectively doctors, dentists and the world of fashion), the stage (acting) or the box (television).

Interesting metaphors come from every imaginable industry. Railways have of course given us *to go off the rails* and carpentry brings *to hit the nail on the head*. Hairdressing provides *wash-leathery* for hair in poor condition, *donkey fringe* for a straight fringe across the forehead, and *kiss curl* for a sculptured curl; electronics language names from their shapes various antennae called *batwings, cheeses, scimitars* and *hulahoops*; and on the shop floor, when unemployment and contraction of industry are discussed, there is a fearful introduction of slaughtering and warfare terms like *get the axe/chop* and *the knives are out*. From the kitchen comes the blunt refusal *I don't boil mi cabbages twice*, i.e. 'I'm not going to repeat myself'. House stairs have *nosings* or *bull-noses* for the rounded fronts of the horizontal sections called *treads*, *stringers* to hold the staircase sides, and *kites* or *kite-winders* for the biggest stairs, which have to be so shaped as to wind round corners. Another delightful comparison* from house-owning (old-style) is *to talk bay-windowed*, i.e. with a polished or affected air. Perhaps soon we shall be hearing *to live treble-garage* and the like: it is marvellous what a desire to be 'one up on the Joneses' can do.

Fishing has also popularised may striking comparisons. Sea terms always seem to have had a special attraction, either going into Standard English (*accost, import, export, get under way, any port in a storm*) or into slang (*half seas over* for drunk, a *dead muzzler* or *nose-ender* for a wind right ahead); or from their very quaintness, like the Welsh *palf*, literally a paw, and Welsh *llwy* literally a spoon, for an oar-blade. The well-known slang term *swinging the lead* for pretending to be ill shows how accurate fishing metaphors are. It is not *dropping the lead* as the landlubber might expect, for the lead if dropped would be swept by the current out of the vertical and consequently the depth could not be sounded.

Textiles have been another plentiful supplier of vivid metaphors. About two-hundred years ago long-winded story-tellers were likened to spinners of yarn, and today we still say *He can spin a yarn*, though generally of a story that is untrue. Short-axis tubes holding spun cotton are *cheeses*. *Slack-drawn-on*, still applied to people, means lethargic and comes from the weaving sheds, where it indicated that the thread

*Noted also on p. 25.

from bobbin to shuttle was not taut. Such people should *get weaving*. A frequent term today is *going through the mill*. In the early twentieth century most millowners and executives had been machine-workers themselves and obviously believed that experience was the best teacher; and, although many of them sent their sons to expensive schools, they afterwards put them to work in their mills to train them for managerial positions. The boys had to start on time and work in every process room for a certain period before they were given a white-collar job. Many people who nowadays use the phrase correctly to mean 'learning the hard way' have no idea of its origin.

Much else needs simplifying. Science suffers from the weight of terms which were drawn from the dead languages, Latin and ancient Greek, in order to give them meanings without irrelevant overtones. Here the naming of biological and botanical species is interesting. All have Latinised or Greek forms but the majority also have common names. Some of these are onomatopoeic (*cuckoo, peewit*); many are descriptive, such as *stick insect, sucker fish*, and *strings* and *wires* for strawberry runners; and some, like *kiwi* and *orang-utan*, have names that have been carried forward through many centuries and for which there are no English equivalents.

Admittedly, some of these common words seem unfortunately chosen — *snoxun*, one name for the foxglove, is hard to say; *pissabed* (*piss-the-bed* sometimes in Scotland) for the dandelion seems uncouth (apparently children were warned not to eat its diuretic leaves in case they wetted their beds at night — cf. French *pissenlit*); and Cumberland's *mammalaikins* for the wood anemone sounds childish. Nevertheless, having common alternatives at hand allows a more satisfactory choice. For example the wood anemone could be called just that, or, as it sometimes is, *bow bells* or *snake's eyes*, all surely preferable in normal conversation to its botanical name *anemone nemorosa*. The cowslip is indeed *primula veris* and the dandelion *leontodon taraxacum*, but surely not to most people. It would be nice if Percy Thrower and the horticultural industry in general could be in a position to speak more clearly and substitute more romantic words.

And how do medical students react to their grotesque language? Most patients, deliberately or otherwise, simplify it. Windpipes and pharynxes can be *throats, guzzles, gullets, gully-'oles, gozzles, wezzens* or *gizzards*; the hip-bone a *yuck-bone, thigh-bone, whirl-bone, hook, haunch, oxter* or *'uggin*; and the groin a *lank, lisk, stifle* or *lock-hole*. Rheumatism may be called just *the pains* as if anyone should know which pains are being referred to; styes on the eye may be *quats* or *wests*; the uvula a *clock*, morphia *murphy*, a stethoscope a *lug-horn*; and so on.

Although science and industry often fail to simplify their language (cf. Chapter 14), at other times, as this chapter shows, they make a brave and vivid attempt. And their struggle towards reasonable simplification merits some support. Specialists communicating amongst themselves no doubt need exact language; but when specialist explains to layman, or officialdom to the general public, something often seems lacking. In the desire to simplify, especially in electronics and computer terms but throughout industry, there might be something for all bureaucrats to bear in mind.

13 'Help' of the Mass Media

Let us now consider the language of the communicators. The reason for such an investigation is that, although few except those living there have to cope, e.g., with Sheffield cutlery terms, Cornish tin-miners' language or the bottle-washing terms of central Birmingham, we are all bombarded with communicators' language via T.V., radio and books, and need some criterion, some defence, to see how near their brands of truth approach universal truth.

A serious criticism is that T.V. should interest itself not just in general work situations but in workers' language, an untapped area. It doesn't go often enough right into the works to see what makes workpeople tick. Football has its well-known language of *goalies, strikers, sweepers* etc. seized on by the media, but in general they seem to have neglected these vast areas of industrial language. T.V. producers in particular, it seems, can't see beyond the end of their lens. Reasons for ignoring it may include the drabness, comparative darkness and difficulties of interrupting work cycles if T.V. crews were to descend regularly into factories, whereas at a first-class soccer match all the ingredients — vast crowds, violent emotions and a colourful outdoor scene — are sizzling away and only need filming. Another important reason is that there seems no one in industry with a great enough interest in communication along with an interest in its possibilities through T.V.

But it is a pity because television is a significant part of national culture, as the background to working life ought to be. Television could be a powerful influence to show the public at large what conditions, hopes and disappointments motivate great sections of industry. It adds faces to work-situations which might be vague and to voices which might be forgotten. Moreover, although on T.V. pomposity and anything false are soon exposed, a sincere attitude or message seems to come across better than on any other medium. Therefore, wherever a section of industry has a genuine grave complaint or a fine achievement of which it is justly proud, what is the sense in keeping it from T.V.?

Newspaper treatment of industry is much kinder, wider and more sensible. When one thinks of the quality of the copy turned out by the average journalist, working some- times on meagre facts, against suspicion, ignorance or misplaced zeal, and always against time, his technical skill should arouse admiration. Millions have enjoyed newspaper items on all sorts of subjects, and been mentally richer for it. They will have the pleasure of reading and discussing many more, all brought into their ken by discerning editors and their staff. Therefore it should be in no spirit of carping criticism or sly superiority that we now detail some of the marks of journalistic language.

Its first objective is to make sure the paper is bought. This is done chiefly by a mixture of ingenuity, suspense and surprise. Evening newspapers come out under a bewildering variety of descriptions, all designed to make the reader believe they come hot from the press. The noon edition will be the *home* or *city edition*; but only an expert like a punter hoping to have picked the *five winners* and ready therefore to pounce on the racing results can sort out the relative priority of *extra, last extra* and *late night final.* Suspense is fostered by newspaper placards announcing e.g. *Cabinet changes, Rates shock, Murder 'hunt development, Star transferred, Big match result.* The object is so to whet the appetite of passers-by that curiosity will make them buy a paper to see who has joined the Cabinet, which player has been trans- ferred, how the match has ended, and so on.

Much surprise is created by startling headlines, with shorter words for greater impact (e.g. *Strike On, Death Fall*). Occasionally the short words chosen prove unintentionally vague or comical — *Police move in book case; Man shot arresting dead man*; or *Books man entices away wife*, which, it transpires, heads a column about an author, not an accountant or bookseller. Much more often, however, the headline embodies skilful play on words — *Just your luck*, the title of an astrology column; *Death of a Queen*, about the last cruise of the liner *Queen Mary; Cut-price cutlery war*; or *Feat with Feet*, about a sponsored walk. Sometimes efficient use is made of contrast (*Best man becomes groom's worst foe*); and there crop up from time to time headlines which are so odd, ambiguous or amusing that the reader wonders whether they have been printed deliberately or by pure accident — *Bury Smallpox Suspects, Boy Grows Foot in 6 Weeks, Singer Smashes All Records, Fish Talks at Fleetwood.*

Newspaper writing has its special techniques. The most important statements generally go into the first paragraphs, so that if necessary during sub-editing the story may be cut from the bottom up (one often feels the same procedure has been adopted with T.V. documentaries). Secondly, as bad news startles more than good news, floods, deaths and catastrophes of all kinds make excellent newspaper material. Although we want to escape them, at their mere mention the true journalist's ears begin to twitch. 'Drivers deliver their usual loads of hardcore to city-centre building site' is no news, but 'Three drunken labourers fall to death after topping-out ceremony' certainly would be. This bias towards bad news makes national dailies criticised for suppressing some items and consequently distorting the rest. Flare-ups of violence are often reported in highly dramatic fashion, but the continuing conflict, because it is continuing and not dramatic or sensational, goes unreported.

National papers are sometimes blamed for sending reporters to pester the family of a dying personality, and producing as soon as he dies an obituary which has been in storage, e.g. at a news agency, ready for the occasion. At local level, this is atoned for by those many papers which go out of their way to ease the lot of the bereaved by printing, instead of something stark like *death notices*, just *Mr R. Smith* or *Obituary*, which by their length, Latinity or apparent vagueness seem kinder.

Popular newspapers are characterised by a visual rather than a verbal appeal, as though digesting only words is the hardest mental grind. Pictures and cartoons will break up the pages — sometimes practically the whole front page will be a picture, and if advertisements are included as much as half the whole 'reading' area may be devoted to pictures. Not only this, but the typography and layout of the pages will pander to the simpler non-verbal approach. Much popular newspaper communication is not language as we know it at all.

Again, the more popular papers concentrate on 'human interest' stories and the personalisation of such hard news as they do present. Instead, say, of a straightforward account of the gradual decay of Lancashire dialect features, comes the rather pathetic photograph of one of the poor dialectologists concerned in that search poring over files of cards, along with the neat caption, 'Mr X in search of the lost Lanky Twang' — made more interesting, perhaps, but highly personalised. Another striking result of this desire for familiarity is the custom, rare twenty years ago, of referring to sportsmen not condescendingly by surnames only, but by their Christian names. Formerly, reporters would grant only outstanding players like 'Dixie' Dean and Stanley Matthews the privilege of a forename; but now not only every star and established first-team player receive it, but young hopefuls on first promotion from the reserves or 'A' team.

Neither a history nor any other written record can have complete objectivity. But often the brevity of newspaper articles and reports, the sensationalisation and personalisation of news characteristic of the populars, leave the reader unable to distinguish between the trivial and the important, floundering in a mass of irrelevant and unrelated detail. Immediacy of context is thought to be served by exaggeration — by the frequent use of grammatical and semantic superlatives, where 'Mr Taylor, one of our top physicists' turns out to be just a conscientious, reasonably successful one — and leads, through the law of diminishing returns, to devaluation of overworked words like *tragedy, disaster, calamity, suffering,* and especially *crisis.* If all the so-called political and economic *crises* were really crises, our nerves would be so shattered that we would hardly be able to totter downstairs and have enough courage to open the morning paper.

All must be topical. Whatever is at this moment on everybody's lips attracts most interest, whereas nothing seems so stale as yesterday's news. Something apparently must be good just because it is new, whether it is a new slang word like *fantabulous,* quickly arrived and soon to go, or a new but untested idea. Newspapers, especially the populars, wishing their readers to consider them up-to-date, copy catch phrases like *have a go*, made popular by entertainers. Sometimes one word may be preferred to another, even though it is less accurate, simply because it is more modern – e.g. *escalate* for increase, *confrontation* for any dispute or argument, and *dialogue* for any discussion. Local weeklies, in their search for topicality, mention as many local events and name as many local people as possible, and thus try to satisfy intense curiosity about current local events. That they generally succeed is well shown by the very sound finances of most of them, in contrast to the very shaky ones of several national dailies. Good or bad, the search for topicality urges the journalist on.

As for the technicalities of newspaper English, use is made of strange titles like *Reader Brown*, very helpful when the reporter does not know whether the writer of the letter to his paper is a Mr, Mrs or Miss. Another feature is the coining of nicknames preceded by *Mr* – *Mr Trumpet* for a well-known trumpeter, *Mr Folklore* for an expert on that subject.

The speed of composition means that journalistic style is closest to spoken English. Short words, sentences and paragraphs are preferred – it is quite common to find a one-sentence paragraph. A most obvious characteristic, springing from the desire for brevity, is the strings of nouns in apposition, like *Industry Pay Rises Burden*. Also common, and again for brevity, are the use of the infinitive instead of the future (*T. V. Star to Wed*); replacing *and* by a comma; and combining many unrelated pieces of information in a single sentence – 'Mr J. Jones, 35-year-old chemist and father of four, won the annual competition for the president's putter'.

More artificial still is the inversion of the normal order of subject and verb – 'Stated Mrs Margaret O'Reilly, 'We've had rats on this estate since March'. It is very usual to decry journalese as always bad, but often (even on the sports pages, like those of the *Daily Telegraph*) it is good. The worst type seems to occur in the sports writing of some local weeklies, where, in a cheap attempt to impress, they pad out their writing with long words, clichés and pompous phrases – 'the batsman heard the death rattle' when he was bowled, or 'the spearhead blasted the spot kick past the helpless writhing custodian' to show that the centre-forward easily converted a penalty.

Despite the influence of other media, it is chiefly through newspapers that new terms and, arguably, ideas are transmitted — e.g. *sputnik* and *boutique* from foreign languages, and from America the vocabulary of the drug sub-culture and the aerospace industry (*aerospace* being itself an example, the *command sequence* of modules being another). It is in dissemination, rather than coining, that the papers are the most influential — the prefixes *mini-*, *midi-* and *maxi-* have all been taken up and used most widely by journalists, and it was the newspapers which introduced to this side of the Atlantic the concepts of *the silent majority* and *technological spin-off*, and the newspapers which popularised the phrase *the technological revolution*.

Advertising and its language have always had a marked effect. The desire to communicate or make known personal wants is one of man's primitive instincts. It led the quacks of Roman times to mark the surfaces of their ointments with messages. To advertise British trades, barbers put up outside their shops striped red-and-white poles and pawnbrokers their three brass balls, whilst in shop windows opticians put enormous spectacles and chemists their gigantic bowls of coloured liquid. Our newspapers now depend on advertising for more than half their revenue, and each year Britain spends on advertising a colossal amount, almost half that spent on state education.

Advertisers' language differs from other commercial and industrial language in a number of ways, firstly in its frequent use of exaggeration — *advertisers' puff*, as it is humorously called. 'Fantastic world première! Colossal attraction!' state the bill-boards, but the experienced theatregoer ignores them and makes up his own mind, having attended other 'world premières' in provincial towns of plays which afterwards just struggled through a fortnight's billing in the West End or never reached there at all. Words for smallness tend to disappear. There are only standard, medium and large eggs. The customer asking for a small tin of ointment is told reproachfully that there are no small tins, only *large, extra large* and *giant size*.

Sometimes commercial language seems snobbish. In a shop, if you are old-fashioned enough to ask for toothpaste, as likely as not this will be tactfully corrected to *dentifrice*, or a request for stockings may elicit the reply, 'Is modom referring to our hose?'. If you state bluntly that you would like the shopkeeper to *chalk it up* or *put it on the slate*, or that you want to pay on *hire purchase* or *on tick* or *on the never-never* (which sounds admittedly worst of all, as if you will never pay), this will meet the rebuke, 'We prefer, sir, to call it deferred payments'.

Much advertising consists of sheer bullying. We are confronted repeatedly by commands like *Buy So-and-So* with no reason given. There is a theory, unhappily often true, that, if you tell people that something is best often enough, they will believe it. Another criticism, this time from teachers, is that some advertisements destroy spelling. Goodness knows, English spelling is often peculiar enough anyway, without further temptations like *Drinka Pinta Milka Day* (government-sponsored too!), *Shellubrication, Beanz meanz Heinz* or *Betta Getta Bretta* (a Lambretta scooter). A third criticism is that other advertisements destroy meaning. The *youth required for butchering* type, so often ridiculed in language textbooks, is no artificial concoction, for it keeps bursting into print. Even the *experienced lady punch operator* type of vacancy advetisement, although it can be shown to cause no real ambiguity, is not couched in the most happily chosen words.

The advertiser, according to the nature of his product, tries to play on all possible basic motives, including the desires for good food and drink, warmth and protection, love, health, beauty and comfort. It is remarkable how much advertising appeals especially to four emotions:

1. Pride (including snobbery, the eagerness to 'put one over those Smiths next door'). Examples of such status-angled advertisements are 'Top people take *The Times*', 'What every well-dressed man is wearing', 'Join the big car set'.
2. *Sex*. Almost every poster advertising a seaside resort shows prominently a bikini-clad girl; cars in advertise-

ments have glamorous models getting into or out of them with some leg difficulty or else sprawled nonchalantly around the bonnet; and even things quite unliked with sex, like crash helmets, are portrayed through it. Refrigerators and washing machines sometimes have captions like 'This will delight the woman you love', accompanied by a picture of a neat, attractive, young housewife (a glamorous model would be out-of-place here) looking admiringly at her husband. The male reader is supposed to think, 'Of course I love my wife, so I should buy her one of those'. Men like to be complemented by women, and the suggestion, subconsciously at least, behind such advertisements is that men buying things like those can have along with them, almost like accessories, women like those. The female figure is the bait to attract attention to the print.

3. *Belonging*, the desire to be one of the crowd, which is stimulated by 'Be sociable, have a Pepsi'; or by 'Beer, a man's drink', to make anyone feel a 'sissy' if he takes only soft drinks. Often the sex and sociability angles are combined, as in the last example or in a 'Yo-Ho-Ho' rum advertisement, which suggests that if you drink, as ordinary sensible poeple do, the beverage concerned, the opposite sex will cluster round you in awe and admiration.

4. *Fear*, e.g. of ugliness, baldness, illness or leaving one's family unprovided for. Thus come many advertisements dealing with health ('Hair restored in two weeks', 'You too can have a body like mine'), and finance ('Save for your children's future').

Among advertisers' methods, legitimate and less so, to whet the basic human emotions, these especially stand out:

1. The slogan remembered through its very simplicity ('Beer is best', 'Put a tiger in your tank'), or through its double meaning ('Players please', which could mean '. . . if you please' or that they please the smoker).
2. Unfinished advertisements, which the reader prides

himself on being able to complete, and in so doing, like anyone taking an active part in anything, becomes greatly interested not just in the words but in the product. Examples are the well-known *Schw. . . .* or *6 million consumed every day* with a picture of some of the bottles, implying that the product is so famous and good that its makers need no mention by name. Similar is *Tetley's bitter men, you can't beat them* ('so join them' understood).

3. References to hoped-for beauty, — *that schoolgirl complexion,* or *you'll be lovelier each day* with a certain toilet soap. It has been found that some women will pay several times the manufacturing price of a bar of soap provided it promises, not only to make them clean, but to be *mild and good for the hands* or *a 7 days' beauty treatment.*

4. Stressing good points and ignoring the not so good — *desirable residence* (desirable perhaps to live in though its high price may be most undesirable); *press the button and we'll do the rest* (highlighting a camera's ease of operation and not its cost); *cheapest radio on the market* (though the cheapness must limit its fineness of tone); *walk-round store* (where the goods are so accessible that you may be tempted to buy far more than you need); or *handy-pack* (stressing its convenience rather than its smallness). A wife, out shopping with her husband, has been known to say, 'Don't take the large economy size: get the small expensive box we can afford'.

    Some of this effect is achieved by euphemisms, gentle terms for unpalatable truths. A van falling to bits will be *elderly,* a man with a 40-inch waist will be *putting on weight a bit,* a woman of similar girth will have a *fuller figure* or just be *rather big.* No goods are merely *cheap* (and by implication worthless), but they can be *less expensive* or *at competitive* or *keenest prices.* For advertiser and purchaser, *Limited Income Clothes for the Mature Figure* sounds better than *Cheap Clothes for Stout Old Women.*

5. A technique or trick, popular with sellers of many doubtful products and services, of claiming testimonials

from unnamed people — 'Thousands of letters extol the merits of our lozenges', 'Mrs J. S. of Norwich writes . . .', 'Many famous personalities come here to have their fortunes told'. Rather similar is the pseudo-scientific approach, bringing in the experience of the apparent expert — 'Doctors [or *chemists, scientists* or *good drivers*] recommend . . .', or the weight of the vast but uncheckable majority — '90 per cent of people use UG'.

6. The method adopted by some firms of comparing their products with those of unnamed rivals, naturally to their own advantage: *X washes whiter, Never know-ingly undersold, The best you'll ever meet.*

7. The personal opening — 'Do you suffer from head-aches?', not 'This is for the benefit of headache sufferers'.

8. Stretching word meanings, notably for cars which have had *virtually one owner*; or are *immaculate*, or in *showroom* or *absolutely mint condition. Older-type* or *traditional* houses or those of *character* are plentiful; but strangely not those — and there must be some — which are *decaying* or *ramshackle*. Estate agents use *modern* for any dwelling built after 1918, and some owner-occupiers have admitted that *post-war* in their advertisements means after the First World War. Food also is not always what it seems to be. Though labelling regulations have improved, *fresh* can be used to describe canned or frozen foods.

9. The implication that goods are being given away — *3p. off* (never on!); *free 200-page colour catalogue*, with its cost included in the price of what it sells; *lard free with every packet of bacon*, but you must buy the bacon; *send no money now*, though later you will have to send plenty. Appeals to the housewife's sense of thrift come in the very names *bargain centre, cut-price shop, economy stores, supermarket.* Note too the frequent questionable use of figures — *Blocked drains cleared from £4.99p.*, on paying which you may be surprised to find that almost £10 has disappeared; or *Houses at £7950*, which with extras approach the £10,000 mark.

Television advertising is far-reaching and very persuasive, especially for those goods like biscuits and chocolates bought usually on impulse. Because the viewer is comfortably settled in his chair, he is more receptive to anything from *the box*, including all the exhortations and commands thrust at him during the commercial channels' 'natural breaks', which occur so often. Chief among television methods are:

1. Repeating the product's name as often as possible in the very brief and costly time allowed — 'Dogs like Doggo. Get Doggo, No dog is a dog without Doggo. Get Doggo now'.

2. The personal approach by means of the bogus interview — 'Why yes', replies the T.V. housewife to the actor-interviewer, 'since I started buying your cereal, the children bounce off to school in high spirits, ready to cope with anything' — all meant to show the ordinary housewife that what suits the T.V. household will suit hers. And there are all the T.V. detergent and cooking 'tests', which only the most gullible person could imagine quite genuine.

3. Suitable background music — hearty pub songs to accompany a certain beer advertisement, dreamy melodies for the 'radiant freshness' of beauty preparations, etc.

4. Contrasting voices — a whispered mention of B.O. (body odour), followed by happy voices when the difficulty has been resolved and love runs smoothly again.

5. Alliteration ('They *t*antalise and *t*i*t*illa*t*e your *t*aste-buds'), puns ('Everybody's *switching*' [to Red Arrow, a make of T.V. set]), and rhyme ('Murraymints, the too-good-to-hurry mints').

However, one sometimes wonders at viewers' credulity. Visitors to one household claimed they were forced to ask their hostess why she plugged the aerial in more tightly after each programme, and asked why. 'I was told it would keep the interference away', she replied 'But we didn't see any', they remarked. 'Of course you didn't', she replied, 'It works very well, doesn't it?' Seriously though, would it be asking too much of television advertisers to give a more accurate picture of life instead of so much exaggeration and mushy sentiment?

According to their own lights, advertisers in all the mass media are very logical. It is no use our grumbling that all forms of advertising — signs, pictures, speech or print— embody some distorting element. So does human nature itself, which is nearly always unfair, hostile or biased in some way. However, these elements tend to cancel each other out; and if an advertiser or communicator cannot get through on one wavelength, he will try another.

Over great regions of advertising, especially about motoring, there must be the temptation to plug, and there is undoubtedly more plugging than impartial advertisement. Surely, for example, T.V. 'housewives' who can't tell margarine from butter must be actresses who have never made a tea in their lives (which seems unlikely), or are just making paid professional statements, or by unhappy coincidence are taste-blind — though the margarine is no doubt excellent value. People, through advertising, are certainly being primed or stimulated into buying, and sometimes conned, e.g. into getting electrical house appliances which are afterwards little wanted, or trousers whose pockets disintegrate after only a year's solid use.

How far the consumer is taken in is a matter of opinion. Commercial ideas — and political ones — are sold ultimately on the value and acceptability of the product. Packaging and advertising will help to introduce them and keep them before the eyes of the public. They may even brainwash a section of the public into thinking for a time that they like what they don't. But finally the man-in-the-street comes back to asking, 'Are these people giving me what I want?' The trouble is that doubtful advertising so often delays his approach to the realisation of truth, and this applies to much of what is distilled by the mass media.

DID YOU NOTICE?

In contrast to advertising language, formal official language as usually disseminated by the mass media seems heartless. The Inland Revenue sends its soulless demands for income tax, the local authorities theirs for rates. The small shopkeeper has to cope with intricate orders about operating Value Added Tax. The layman does not fully comprehend religious language and certainly not that of the law, which is why the *New English Bible* has appeared and why a commission is inquiring into legal language. The resulting queries, objections, appeals and arguments breed confusion and often intense hatred of the language of officialdom.

It is refreshing, therefore, to find informal notices on doors of offices and factories which often provide unexpected or humorous comment contrasting strongly with formal official language. They modify — and at times improve — the mechanical impersonal world of administrators. We object to announcements like 'Senior Personnel Only' unless we come into that category; and 'Drive carefully — elderly persons crossing' somehow seems wrong with *persons* for the more human *people*. It is hard to keep a happy medium between the too heavy and threatening and the too flippant, but sometimes a lighter tone does no harm.

Some of these notices are deliberate — 'I am free whenever my secretary says I am' (from an overworked boss). Others are the effusions of unknown wags: 'Out of order — by order'; We will accept anything in exchange, even your mother-in-law'; 'Only old crocks admitted' (at a hospital); 'Beware of cat'; 'Danger — photonic radiation' (on a light switch); 'No smoking — even if you are the boss's relation' (seen in an antique-cum-junk shop). Similar was 'duck or grouse' over one of the low entrances to Manchester's Grand Hotel kitchens. Like slang, they are all attempts to humanise.

An opposite type of notice is the unintentionally comic or absurd, such as: 'Only authorised personnel are authorised to use this equipment' (on a fire-fighting appliance at an Air Force base in Suffolk); toilet paper printed *Government Property* or *reconditioned*; a box observed for over a year on waste land in Middlesbrough, pleading 'Church Restoration Fund' and surrounded by a heap of rubble. Other unintentional examples are: 'Antiques — lunch here'; 'Ice-cold drinks inside', on a shop window full of sexy magazines; 'Post-mortem room — ring for attention'; and 'New Diversion', on a lamp-post bent by the impact of a car. From a Northern second-hand shop shortly before demolition came 'Removals undertaken. Estimates given. Moonlight flits* a speciality'; and at Padstow in Cornwall a public convenience sign was photographed directing the public straight into the harbour.

Car auctions are good hunting grounds for notices and claims which are serious to buyer and apparently seller but humorous to the bystander: e.g. 'Ford popular, 4 sound tyres, new clutch, very clean, no tax, no warranty, no M.O.T., good runner, a snip at £50', which the auctioneer has to have started with the aid of an enormous battery boost. Amusement lies too in considering why certain notices have been redrafted. In an amended notice about bus stopping times came the alarming statement, 'London Transport does not guarantee that its services . . . will run at all', although it generously added that it would try to keep them going. In another, it changed 'Smokers are requested to occupy rear seats' to 'Smokers are asked to sit at the back'. Was the first version hard to understand, or was it ambiguous, with smokers believing they could occupy seats by sprawling, lying, or jumping up and down upon them? Smokers are evidently difficult to reason with. Hull buses have just had inserted 'Please' before their notices 'Do not smoke', on which apparent lightening of regulations Hull smokers have been puffing away more furiously than ever.

A third type of extraordinary notice is that which crazily defies accepted spelling. It is very frequent in corner-shop windows, but is met in newspapers and elsewhere. Thus: 'No appoyntment nessessery' (at a high-class hairdresser's); or, displayed in a quiet guesthouse, 'This dinning room is out of bounds to none residents after 6.30'; or, 'Lost, Wed., green buggerigar, answers to Jackie'.

Wayward apostrophes cause a fourth type. Any survey of a working-class shopping area will soon reveal notices like those of butchers with their 'prime cut's' and cafés boasting 'chip's with pie's and pea's'. More serious, because of its place of origin, was a notice on a school door announcing 'Infant's Kitchen', as if one infant there was a real glutton. Still more public is a large misplaced stone apostrophe on a deserving

---

*Hurried removals at night, to escape creditors.

"childrens' mission" building in Wood Street, Manchester, which has apparently stood there for almost seventy years. Other mechanical errors have led, through wrong word order, to notices of the 'Lost, woolly lady's cardigan' type; and apparently from a reporter's telephone mishearing, the giant-killing F.A. Cup attraction of Leeds travelling to play the railwaymen's institute team, Horwich (for *Norwich*).*

Mistakes like those above do add variety. So in this area at least, through traces of deliberate and unintentional humour, the language of public communication may take on a human dimension.

*Manchester Evening News, 13 Jan. 1973.

14 More Problems

Handicaps to understanding industrial language are numerous. One is the speed of talk, which changes wildly according to mood and context. A Standard English speaker uses in normal conversation about 120 words a minute, but factory talk can be agonisingly slow or breathtakingly fast. The works thinker can add immensely to his reputation by slowly dropping into an argument an occasional *aye, nay, oh?* or *mebbe.* On the other hand, words can fly out fast. This is partly through excitement — if a workmate drops an axe on your toe, you won't search delicately for the most semantically accurate word, or check etymological derivations before letting loose a suitable reply. Quick talk is also caused by the frequent habit of bashing words together. To see how good you are at this, let's try a test. To stop yourself cheating, as you translate, first cover the right-hand column. Two marks for an all-correct line, one for one word wrong, and *nowt* for less than that:

Standard Factory Language	*Standard English*
1. WOSSUPPAL?	What is the matter, friend?
2. BERRAGERRALORRABIGUNS	You would be advised to obtain many big ones.
3. WOSSITLIKE?	How are conditions?
4. GROUTNSHURRUP	Get out and be quiet.
5. LERRUSGERRARIM	Let me get at him.
6. AV BROU' A BI' O' BE'ER BU'ER	I've brought a bit of better butter.
7. FIRRITINEER	Fit it in here.
8. GAFFERSOFFISNUT	The managing director is crazy.

Scoring. Full marks — you are a model British worker.
8—15 — you are learning. Keep it up.
Below 8 — consider whether you are, or would be, a loose cog in industry.

To qualify for the advanced diploma in workaday speech, you should be adept, not only at drawling, or at spitting out words like maching-gun bullets as just tested, but in repartee,

127

the art of making quick clever replies to turn the tables on someone asking an awkward question. When ordered to do something you dislike, you can counterattack with 'What about you?', 'Think I'm a mug?', or, pointing to your eyes, 'See any green here?'. If asked for something foolish, you can say, just as irresponsibly, 'Talk daft and I'll buy your coalyard' or, 'I had one but the wheels came off'.

Understatements are a little puzzling. *Not so bad* usually means quite good. The Yorkshire worker who is *middlin'* is fairly well, but *nobbut middlin'* is rather poorly. The miner has a capacity for deliberate understatement which adds strength to his remarks. When the Duke of Edinburgh visited one of the Astley collieries in the 1950s, he so satisfied the miners with his shrewd questions and man-to-man behaviour that one of them was moved to say to the local press, 'He's no stone jug, yon mon'. This was the highest possible praise from a South Lancashire miner, and bestowed only upon outstanding performers. Joe Louis, Bradman and Epstein would just about have measured up to it.

But exaggerated comparisons can puzzle even more. In Standard English we have some hyperbole in metaphors, but they are now well known and their meanings clear — we talk of a *sea of faces, splitting hairs*, the *last straw that broke the camel's back, speaking volumes*, the *right hand not knowing what the left is doing*, or *driving a coach and six* through a set of regulations. More surprising are the apparently unorthodox similes a worker takes from his own environment. The miner is a good example. Instead of the standard 'as cunning as a fox', he prefers 'as cunning as an overman'. Similarly he uses 'as daft as a prop' because the pit-prop can be *squozen* (squeezed) to death without feeling a twinge; 'thick as a chock'; 'legs like pit-props'; 'as deaf as a roadnail' (for nailing sleepers to underground rails); 'as dry as a stick'; 'as tough as rock', since he meets that more than leather; 'as weak as smoke', from shot-firing and offering no resistance, or 'as weak as water', which drips from the mine roof.*

The grim terseness of many Northern workmen's remarks seems to reflect the characteristics of their Viking ancestors. They show a liking for lugubrious comparisons — 'to marry

*Also Biblical; see Ezek. 7:17 and 21:7.

t'midden for t'muck', 'her face is like the back of a bus', 'he clams (=starves) his belly to feed (=clothe) his back', 'mi belly thinks mi throat's cut'. But startling exaggerated comparisons are not the monopoly of the North. They are widespread in British working and general language. That is why we get colourful phraseology like, 'He'll swear through an inch board', 'as clever as three blokes — two fools and a madman', 'it's like stopping an oven with butter' (of a useless effort), 'he's loose in the haft' (i.e. foolish or unreliable); and why the motorist, having hastily found an illegal parking spot, refers angrily to the traffic warden, who books him, as a disease, *yellow peril*.

Here, for general instruction and enjoyment, is a typical selection of exaggerated comparisons: 'As thrunk (crowded) as three in a bed': 'legs like matchsticks'; ''e couldn't push a 'ole in a echo'; 'he can't knock the skin off a custard', 'as daft as a brush' (which flops, unable to stand upright); 'hold your water' ('don't get excited'); 'he's fair bow-legged with brass' (very rich); 'if he had any more mouth, he'd have no face to wash'; 'if he fell off the Co-op, he'd fall in the divi'. Football grounds provide their extreme ones, like 'Offside a mile!', impossible because of the length of the pitch; and 'You black sod' — inaccurate description of the referee, colourwise and in other respects. Two gems from Liverpool dockland conclude this assortment — 'De 'ouse is alive wid dead rats' and 'he's got a nose on him as long as the Corporation housing list'.

It is surprising that works language gets away with such exaggerated comparisons when in other spheres, as magistrates well know, any attempts to 'gild the lily' are usually recognised as signs of untruth which do their speakers no good at all. There seems to be one law for the law courts, with their unending quest for absolute truth, and another for factories and the like, where different shades of truth live quite happily together.

Lying, white and black, are other blocks to full understanding, provided the reader or listener doesn't see through the deception — 'Must close now to catch the post', for 'Can't think how to end this awkward letter'; 'Just half a cup' ('Fill it up'); 'Very interesting talk' ('Couldn't understand a word of it'), 'We're just looking round' ('Let's get out — these prices are sky-high'), 'We were just passing' ('We came ten miles out of our way to catch you'); 'Very sorry, I seem to have no change' ('Flag days should be abolished').

Vagueness, deliberate or accidental, is another hindrance to understanding what management or workers mean. Deliberate vagueness, putting a mild for a blunt expression, is called euphemism. It is a lie or half-truth made chiefly in three ways:

1. By introducing a foreign word which is less well known and so less offensive, e.g. *lingerie* for underclothes or *maniac* for madman. Similarly *aroma* or *odour* for what the ordinary British workman would call a *stench*, *pong* or *stink*.
2. By substituting a vaguer English term for a more precise one — *excess, lapse, offence, misconduct, slip* or *transgression* for rape, bigamy, housebreaking, murder or other crime; *he has a very direct manner* for 'he's extremely rude.'
3. By resorting to the negative — *unwise* for foolish, *unclean* for dirty, *unsafe* for dangerous, *impolite* or *discourteous* for rude.

Some euphemisms seem kindly — thus *senior citizens* or *O.A.Ps* for old age pensioners, for no one wants to be branded by the weekly act of drawing public money, usually before the gaze of any curious Post Office customer, even though the money may have been earned over many years. When the working mother tells her young children that someone has died, the favourite expression is *he's gone to sleep*; when they ask about the facts of life, she claims that the stork brings babies, or that they are found under a gooseberry bush. Many euphemisms intended for adults, however, are so exaggerated as to be plain ridiculous. Observe the *rodent operator*, who was once a rat-catcher; or the *transparent wall maintenance engineer*, the title on whose van suggests he is at least a master glazier but who proves to be a window-cleaner. Others, though not ridiculous, sound a trifle unreal. Do you, for instance, know exactly who all these are? — *saleslady, modiste, turf accountant, water department officer, coiffeur, flueologist?* Would you prefer to patronise a *chippie, fish-oil* or *seafood restaurant?* Are some people *deaf* or just *hard of hearing*, and others poor or just *financially embarrassed?* Are goods stolen or *dishonestly acquired* or simply *knocked off?* The basic differences are really only of language.

Official euphemisms abound. Backward countries have become *underprivileged* or *developing nations.* Slums seem to have gone; but in their places we have *clearance areas*; streets of *twilight houses*, and city centres *ripe for redevelopment.* Crime, say the police, is increasing, but in official parlance it is on the wane, because habitual criminals are just *persistent offenders*, and imprisonment is (mildly) *preventive detention*, possibly in a contradiction called an *open prison.* The popular dailies and Sunday newspapers have given undertones to *assault, commit an offence*, and *interfere with*; adultery is just *misconduct* or the cosy-looking *intimacy.* On reading 'Shortly after the murder, a man was at the station helping police with their inquiries', we know he is unlikely to have gone there volunteering to help. On roads, people are *fatally injured* rather than killed, even when death is instantaneous; and trains or important pieces of information are *delayed*, not *late.*

Hard though it may be to comprehend, the government has been highly successful in ridding the country of unemployment, and certainly of the old-fashioned dole queues like those of the early thirties. Nevertheless, hundreds of thousands are very familiar with *redundancy* caused by *recession; supplementary benefit*; and the need for *superfluous labour* in the *underprivileged regions* (the former distressed areas), if they cannot eke out their *national assistance*, to submit to *redeployment*, a name which appears almost laudable but means tearing up home roots because of forced transfer.

Foreign students in the English degree-making factories have become imperceptibly *overseas students*, which stirs confusion with those from Australia, for example, and especially from Ireland, so that for examination purposes they sometimes have to be designated, most awkwardly, *non-native speakers of English.*

In industry, the politely termed *merger* may hide the fact that a bankrupt or badly-run firm is being swallowed by a more profitable one regardless of shareholders' interests, and

a widely-heralded *take-over* 'success' is all too often an
attempt by a large firm of moderate efficiency to buy
without properly working for them the profits of a more
efficient business. In industry, as elsewhere, things are not
always what they seem! Still at the official level, we often
hear of *industrial collisions* or *disputes* rather than strikes,
and of the workers' *rest and refreshment period reorganised*
instead of their dinner break being cut; constantly both
nationalised and private concerns have to *review, revise* or
adjust their prices — but always in one direction, upwards;
and people are not dismissed, but *given notice* (which sounds
less cruel), *asked to leave, requested to resign, relieved of
responsibilities, have their employment terminated*, or are
merely *considered redundant*.

Parallel with official euphemisms come shop-floor ones.
Goods are not stolen but *requisitioned* (Forces' term from
the Second World War), *knocked off* (but not accidentally),
pinched or in rhyming slang *half-inched,* or else *nicked.*
Workers, like management, believe they can't be dismissed;
but they fear getting *the push, the boot, their cards* or *the
sack.*

Some occupations may need disguising — the undertaker
does not advertise clearly what he undertakes to do. But an
amazing battery of elegant terms provides people in most
walks of life with a means of rising quickly in apparent
status, if not so much financially. An office boy is a *junior
clerical assistant*, his immediate boss may find himself an
executive officer. A small-town moneylender blossoms into a
financier; we have *kitchen-waste operatives* and *fenestro-
logists*; and people working in the city in any minor or menial
capacity are *in business.* Town clerks, however, have had a
rather degrading title, since in many ways they are the most
important local men, and more permanent than councillors,
aldermen or mayors. Some town clerks — probably very
suitably — have become *Directors of Administration*; but
simultaneously below them have appeared *Directors of Parks,
of Lighting, of Sanitation*, and so forth. Perhaps behind some
of these changes lies a desire to upgrade their jobs in order to
profit in any wide amalgamation of local governments.

There is a creditable desire to play down success, which is another reason for understatement or euphemism. Farmers are notorious for never admitting to be enjoying good years. There is a long-standing joke, which must have some bearing on practice, about an interviewer saying to an old farmer, 'Yes, but apart from import tariffs, low price of beef, blight, foot-and-mouth disease, taxes and floods, are you getting on all right?' To operate the understatement technique by qualifying instantly any success is quite easy — if congratulated on a fine show of goods you say, 'Yes, but customers'll not want 'em'; if you win the treble chance, 'Not so bad, but luck'll soon even up and inflation'll soon wreck it'; if you rapidly recover from a mild bout of flu, 'I'll try to struggle up. I might just mucky another clean collar.'

There are also the very useful all-purpose words *uncle, aunt* and *friend*. The *uncle* who becomes known to a child may be a relation, a good friend of the family, or occasionally the mother's new lover. A *friend* can be of either sex and any age, and can imply more than mere friendship — 'We're just good friends' is the stock answer to inquiries about the relationship of well-known people, and sometimes it is wise not to inquire further. Anything disagreeable tends to be given a kindlier name. Thus a *heart condition* is a poor one; and we notice male colleagues who are said to be *getting on a bit, elderly, putting on weight* or with *middle-aged spread*, but never old, rotund or obese, and women who are just *tall* or *big*, not plump or fat.

Places, too, acquire politer names. The slaughterhouse has turned into the *abbatoir*. No longer do people go to the old-fashioned *netty, nessy* or *privy*. They started going instead to the *W.C., toilet,* or *out back* or *down the yard* without stating a specific destination (the last expression is still used by customers of some Northern pubs with indoor sanitation). More recently have come *conveniences* and *loos*, but, as fast as the meaning of one awkward term becomes known, the search starts for another to replace it. The old *madhouse* is a case in point. It became *bedlam* (from *House of Bethlehem*, from which we get the saying *it's absolute bedlam*), then *lunatic asylum*, from false association with phases of the moon, then *mental hospital*, and now, doubtless to the annoyance of staff and patients in other hospitals, just *hospital*. So euphemisms multiply.

Some abbreviations are designed, not chiefly for shortness, but to hide embarrassing meanings. The *O.A.Ps* have been mentioned. Notice also *B.O.* in advertisements to ward off body odour, and *K.O.*, not as a normal abbreviation for kick-off time, but for a knock-out, since no one likes to admit to the shame and possible brain damage of being on the receiving end of a knock-out blow. Here are some other euphemistic abbreviations: how many can you decipher? — *R.I.P., O.S., R.D.* (when used in banking), *N.G., U.S., B.F.* (a term of abuse).

So this is an outstanding difficulty of occupational and indeed all language — that often the words we use are those we prefer, not those that more dangerously tell the bald truth.

Truth is also obscured, but this time unintentionally, by clichés, which are expressions which through sheer overwork have lost their exactness and impact. We meet many cases of a *crucial decision, unique offer* (when others closely resemble it), *an outstanding sportsman, to be perfectly frank* (Mr Harold Wilson's favourite), *not to worry!*, operating on a *shoe-string budget*, in politics a *whistle-stop tour*, in so many Western films *they went that away*, or the trite remark *It's a small world*.

Another obstacle is tautology, the useless or ineffective repetition of the same idea in different words — *to all intents and purposes, cool, calm and collected, first and foremost, rules and regulations, ways and means, law and order. At this moment of time* is a favourite term. Many people still cautiously ask for a *loaf of bread* as if it might be something else, whilst fishermen talk of a *dan buoy* for what they could easily call just a dan or a buoy.

In contrast to the simplifying tendency described in Chapter 12, exemplified by *tweeters* and *whoofers*, we sometimes prefer a little technicality — e.g. about various *cuts* in suiting or at the hairdresser's — because we feel flattered to receive specialist attention. But there are now appearing some truly difficult terms for the average person to understand. Many of these have been started by zealous followers of a particular hobby, proud apparently that they know far more about it than the general public. Thus coin-collectors have coined for themselves the word *numismatists*, people who study birds are *ornithologists*; and those who study moths or butterflies are *lepidopterists*. If the word *tegistologist* baffles you, ask someone who collects beer-mats.

On the other hand, *cruxverbalists* for crossword-puzzle addicts and *insulaphiliacs* for lovers of islands are word-coinages that have made no impact because, although many people fit these categories, no societies cater for them. But attempts are regularly made to replace old terms by much more difficult new ones. According to reports of a recent Commons debate on urban congestion, Mr Peyton, Minister of Transport Industries, wished to resuscitate the old tram under the name *segregated track vehicle*. Will a conductor say, 'Get the segregated track vehicle out, lad?'

A minor hindrance can be language repetition, but inevitably there has to be a certain amount of this in the working world. It occurs particularly where apprentices are learning customary procedures, and where actions and accompanying words amount to a drill, as in the radio operator's *Over and out*.

Then there are all the space-fillers which are useful in giving anyone a few seconds longer to think what to say next, but which in so many mouths are a real curse, chopping conversations into indigestible bits. *You know* and its Northern equivalent *sithee* are the prime offenders; but there are also all the tail-questions: *Don't you?; Isn't he?*, etc.; *I mean to say; You see?; Right?*, — very popular with Army instructors; — *like*, as in *quietly-like* and *suchlike*; and the meaningless *thingamigig* and *thingamibob*. If only we could think a little more quickly, we could do without a host of these.

Another custom which looks the same but is rather different is that of extending a word nonsensically to make it look more elaborate. A good example is *shandrydan*, originally a farmcart but now used of any vehicle, especially a broken-down one, as 'I don't think much of that old shandrydan'.

The vague language of poorer commercial correspondence is met in many ways. Stock situations bring out conventional references like 'Yours to hand of even date', *inst.* for this month, *prox.* for next month, and old-fashioned ridiculously polite answers like 'We beg to acknowledge your esteemed favour of the 14th ult.'. But by replying the writer is acknowledging receipt, he has no need to beg abjectly, the *favour* here is a letter, and to understand *ult.* the recipient's mind has to work ponderously through unnecessary stages ('*Ult.* is short for *ultimo* meaning 'last', i.e. last month. We're now in March, so last month was February. I've got it! He means 14 February'). Characteristics of this outmoded commercialese are:

1. Circumlocution ('I will cause inquiries to be instituted').
2. Unnecessarily long, abstract, classical or unfamiliar words — goods are *purchased* and *despatched* not 'bought' and 'sent'; people are *communicated with*, not 'told'; delivery will be *expedited,* not 'hurried'.
3. Phrases for single words (*in the great majority of cases* for 'most often').
4. Padding (*It is true to say that . . . .*).

This poorer-type commercial language springs from laudable attempts to be impartial and courteous, though its antique wording makes it fail. Less praiseworthy is another motive behind it, the desire to impress, resulting in strangely pathetic contradictions like these:

We have great pleasure to inform you that the seats you requested are no longer available.

We are afraid that we cannot supply the information you say that you urgently seek. Assuring you of our best attention at all times, we are . . . .

Commerical correspondence can actually block meaning. The highly intelligent and successful owner of a Northern road-haulage concern, had with his wife created the business from nothing by working all hours (this was before the government imposed maximum lorry-driving hours per day).

On its nationalisation, he was compensated but retained as manager. Face-to-face or over the phone he could instruct his drivers perfectly and knew the job from A to Z, but he had to be taught to write intelligible business letters. His office staff in outlying depots were worse, and he had to keep ringing them up to ask what their letters meant. Fantastic though these may seem, they are not isolated examples.

The unfortunate receiver of some business letters is tempted to make his own translations, thus:

"The matter is receiving attention" means 'I'll probably look at it some time'.

'The matter is now receiving urgent attention' means 'We have lost the file'.

'We are making exhaustive inquiries' means 'We'll delay you as long as humanly possible'.

'Thank you very much for your further esteemed favour' means 'We are getting tired of your complaints. Go and pester someone else.'

The best method in commercial correspondence is to write courteously but directly in plain English, the kind so serviceable for reports, memoranda, notices and the like. Write sincerely what seems necessary, without old-fashioned business jargon, and the tone of the letter will take care of itself.

Although antiquated commercialese, with its persistent dread of committing itself, is directly opposed to the honest bluntness of factory-floor language, it is by no means the only kind of misleading professional jargon. Look at barristers' fawning law-court expressions (*I'm much obliged, Your Honour; If your Lordship pleases: With the greatest respect*). Financial writers are much given to 'elegant variation'. Share prices, which basically can only rise, fall or stay level, are not among the most interesting matters linguistically until the journalists play with them — when they start to *jump, leap, waver, retreat, go back, sag* etc. Sometimes, in their search for individual comment, these writers tie themselves into knots. One of them stated of a hotel share: 'It certainly looks as if the risk reward ratio favours the upside rather than the downside potential by a useful margin' — which meant, as far as one can gather, that he believed the shares would some time rise strongly. Of course, financial writers have always to beware of the law of libel, which is why they seem incurably optimistic. Even where they suspect gigantic fraud, they will go no farther than stating, for example, that the shares are *high enough* and *devoid of merit*.

Ambiguity is no help in any trade or profession. Medical terminology with its many Latinised expressions is very exact, as it has to be; but, when patients speak of their complaints in ordinary English, difficulties can arise. In Lancashire, experienced nurses have been puzzled by what sounds like *a pain in th'eye* but proves to be a *pain in th'thigh*; and a doctor practising in Yorkshire, who had previously worked in Cornwall and then Scotland and so should have been well experienced in linguistic problems, records that he kept getting into trouble with his patients by telling them they were *better*, by which he meant 'improving, progressing satisfactorily', but which in their dialect they interpreted as 'fully recovered'.

Avoided words set other problems. Although it is said that our minds helpfully make us remember good times and forget the bad, the reverse can happen, as when workers refer to *being on nights* but have no expressions for the more pleasant daytime shifts.

Words ignored can be most significant. Whereas the layman thinks of miners going down a mine, with few exceptions the older worker himself, getting the coal with pick and shovel, knew he was a *collier* down a *pit*. *Collier* seems to have come from a former need to distinguish coalminers from tin-miners and salt-miners, though before pit-head baths were built coalminers with their blackened faces were unmistakeable as they walked home. In the North-East, the underground worker is usually a *pitman*, although the official term *miner* is starting to replace it, and his language is *pitmatick*. Another case of official terms being ignored is that in January 1965 the National Coal Board was recommending slag-heaps to be known as *spoil-heaps*; but miners, who ought to know, perversely keep referring to them as *(pit-) tips*, *pit-rooks* and *dirt-rooks* (Lancashire),* *pit-'ills, pit-'eeaps, dirt-'eeaps, batches* (Somerset), *bonks* (N. W. Midlands), or in Scotland *bings*.

Some words have died because of changed conditions: thus the modern miner works in a *gang*, no longer in a *pair* as happened in shallow pits, or in a *team*. Still other words are avoided out of superstition. At sea it is taboo to mention *pig* in case the ship should sink and her crew drown — presumably because a pig is one of the few animals which can't swim.

Another great language barrier to the layman is the number of alternatives often current for one idea. In electrical engineering, the earth connection is the *earth, ground* or *deck*. The second is from American and the third from the Fleet Air Arm, but all are now in general use — e.g. 'Where's the earth?', 'It's at ground', 'Tie that lead to deck'. Leads are also *wires* (e.g. in periodicals like *The Radio Constructor*) or *lines*. Valves may also be tubes, from American usage; or *bottles*, often for big output valves compared derisively with neat transistor valves, but also generically for any valves. The part of a factory or mill devoted to one process is in electrical engineering and steelmaking an *isle* or *bay*; but in textiles an *alley* or *gate* from the Old Norse word for road. Thus the *cut alley* for the space in front of looms where the *cuts* are taken off; the *beam alley* behind them; and the *loom-gate, jinny-gate, mule-gate* or *wheel-gate* for the pathway between pairs of spinning machines.

Workmates may be *butties* as in Somerset and South Wales, or *mates, pals*; in Scotland *nibbers*; or in Cumberland, Westmorland and the North-East *marrers*. Waste material of different kinds that they encounter goes under many names. Broken glass may be *fret* or *grog*: in chemical engineering unidentified deposit is *crud* or *crawl*; or if gluey *slutch*, or around Sheffield *gobbo*; and builders' rubbish in general may be *ket, kelderment*, or *drabble*, the last of which is also the unfortunate surname of a most reputable Derbyshire builder.

Tools are apt to acquire very different names. For 'crowbar' we find *pinch(er), ringer, rook*, and *till-iron*. bradawl is

*Cf. *EDD ruck*, sb[4] 3.

quite commonly a *pricker, bodger* or *brog*; and a pavior's
mallet becomes a *tup, mell* or *maul*. A distinguished country
periodical,* which seems to know the language of these
gentlemen, has published a cartoon of an angry foreman
brandishing his fist at a startled labourer, who has dragged all
the rest of the gang from their work, and saying, 'Didn't I tell
you to bring a maul?'. By historical rather than whimsical
twists of the tongue, pincers often become *pinsons* or
pinchers, and a winch turns into a *wince*. A steelyard (the
weighing balance) can be an *auncel, bismar* or *troy*. The
upright of a ladder can be a *limber*, its steps *slotes*, or its rungs
*bars, lats, proons, rails, rances, rims, rounds, spars, spindles,
spokes, staffs, stales, stave(r)s, stays, steals, stowers* or *treads*.
That surely is a list to daunt any rational being. But *Bring
Monday* for a tool is no impossible order, for it refers in
South Lancashire to a 28-lb. hammer which, through the
great exertion needed to wield it, brings you back to your
senses when you return to work on Monday.

What the *New English Dictionary* calls a 'deaf nut' may be
a *dumb nut* and the screw of a thread the *mash*. Coagulated
grease sometimes hides under the names *bleck, betch* or
coom. A workman's leather bag may be a *budget, wallet,
work-poke* or *sack (this last is also used around Nelson for a*
school satchel); whilst for rubbish and associated matters
there is a wild collection of words, including *mullock, prowt,
rammel* and *squit* for rubbish itself, *swarf* that falls from a
lathe (contrasting with the official word *trimmings*); and
shoredrak and *sraftip* for a rubbish-tip.

Some occupational names show disturbing variety, such as
flusherman for the man who works in sewers, *graduate* for a
physician ('He must be bad – a graduate's been to him'),
glasser, glassiver or *glazzener* for a glazier, or *ganger, gang-
drover, gang ('s)man, gangmaster*; and a host of unprintable
names for the foreman or head of a gang of workmen. Added
to this are those queer names beloved of certain broadcast
programmes, where guesses have to be made about the
occupation of a man who introduces himself, e.g. as a *maggy*.
He is actually a man who unloads fish at the quayside in the

*Dalesman (1972 Annual).

early morning, but many ports call him a *lumper, bobber* or *dock-walloper.*

Occupational illnesses have special names. Well known are *housemaid's knee, writer's cramp, tennis elbow* and *athlete's foot*; whilst the welder gets *arc-eyes.* Mining, however, seems to have most. The old collier was very prone to *miner's chest* (pneumoconiosis) from coal-dust settling on his lungs, an increased danger for modern face-workers when even more dust is thrown up by machines. Fortunately rare now is *miner's worm* (hookworm), a horrible complaint caused by intestinal parasites bred by hot moist underground conditions. Less frequent too, because of better conditions, are *beat knee* and *beat elba*, water on the knee or elbow caused by constantly banging them through having to lie sideways hacking at a mine roof in a confined space. But many old miners when subjected to a bright light suffer painfully from *staggy* (ny*stag*mus), bad vision with bloodshot oscillating eyeballs, caused by sand or grit in the eyes. *Staggy* has spread beyong the mining industry: of an incompetent football referee the Lancashire miner will claim *Yon bugger's getten staggy.*

Shift and watch names are among the many terms which seem puzzling and remarkable to an outsider, but to their users quite ordinary expressions. Old fishermen used to work a vividly named system of watches — *light moon flood, light moon ebb,* etc. —* the most hated being the *dark moon ebb,* a watch undertaken in the dark dreary hours of early morning. North-East miners worked a three-shift system of *fore-shift* (4-11 a.m.), *back shift* (9.30-4 p.m.), and *neight shift* (2-9 p.m.), which, despite its name, was worked in the afternoon and evening, not the night. Other arresting shift names include the Nottinghamshire miners' *egg n' bacon shift* (10 a.m.-6 p.m.). so called because it allowed time for a good breakfast before starting work; and the Lancashire *dark days,* humorously for the night shift. In the West Riding two miners, including the deputy, would work the *snifting-shift,* smelling for *gob-stink,* the odour given off by the spontaneous heating of coal — ordinary terms down the mine but

*See the unscripted fishing conversation in Chapter 15.

hardly permissible above ground in polite circles. Bus crews work most complicated shifts, like the *early two-timer* (e.g. 6-10 a.m. and 12 noon-4 p.m., both periods within the traffic day), the *three-timer*, occasionally a *four-timer* (with four duty periods spread over at least nine hours), and the *semi-late* (finishing 7.30-8.45 p.m. and allowing the crew to *sink a pint* before going home). *Doing a ghoster* ('night-shift') is most unpopular, e.g. in electrical engineering; and other hated shifts in that industry are the *rag-time* or *spare-shift*, one necessary to make up the required number of hours for the week, and the *twilight*, a name given by trainees to their 'night school' attendance.

The spawning of many new computer terms can be deceptive. *Hardware* for permanent computer equipment, *software* for the paperwork, and *live ware* for the computer operators have already been mentioned. The last is an Americanism sneaking over here, and typically American in thinking from the computer's viewpoint. Another American term gaining ground over here is *firm ware*. This stands for a computer programme so firmly established that it is almost impossible to change, like one now set in a Manchester computer which, with the connivance of all other senior members of staff, on the day the boss retires is destined to print continuously — and nothing short of a fire or maniacal axe-wielding destruction will stop it — 'Goodbye, you silly old b—'. Puzzling too can be special local technical expressions which sometimes strive for wider recognition, like *bones* and a cluster of other curious variants for the boning rods to measure trench excavations, which in the late sixties certain Somerset schools sent to astonished Northern woodwork examiners.

Spelling is not the communication barrier one might expect. Occasional spellings like *thru, color* and *sulfuric* are accepted as Americanisms caused by much scientific literature and many textbooks being written on the other side of the Atlantic — probably useful improvements, though not yet permissible in normal British writing.

Commercial advertisers run the risk of being pilloried for destroying children's spelling with their *nu* for new, *U* for you, etc.; but, as nearly all shop-floor language is spoken,

very few spelling problems arise there. It will tolerate homo-
phones (words of similar sound) so long as their meanings
differ — no one, on being told to *get the key*, is going to
travel to a harbour and start chopping up a quay to bring it
back. Where a Standard-English-speaking stranger might be
confused by historical change of vowel, the local occupational language keeps words distinct. For example, on the
Yorkshire coast, where the *beetsters*, as they are called, *beet*
nets instead of mend them, there is no mix-up with 'to beat',
for that locally is *beeat*. And occupational language can even
corroborate our seemingly chaotic English spelling — Brix-
ham fishermen, speaking of *calm water* sound the *l* rather as
it must once have been sounded in our standard language;
and this makes sense of the dictionary spelling.

Industrial geography is another matter, and here we do
have a problem. It can start as the worker rises bleary-eyed
and draws the curtains to mutter, 'It's looking bad over our
Jack's house' instead of 'rain seems imminent from the
south-west'. There is additionally the involved question of
whether you go *up* or *down* to London or to Glasgow, which
seems to depend on railway up and down lines, north and
south on the map, and on which city is thought more
important. From Manchester, say, would you go *up, down,
across, over* or just *to* Sheffield? This kind of thing has for
years been worrying Americans in their language surveys of
the U.S.A., but perhaps in Britain we'd better not pursue this
thought-track: it's too complicated.

More important is how local directions are given, and here
any transport worker would make a poor geography teacher,
though what he says may be clearer than formal directions.
It's: 'Go past Robinson's (local bakery), and just past the
island (roundabout), turn left at Dick Kerr's (even though the
firm has long ago been taken over, first by A.E.I. and then by
G.E.C.), and it's two minutes past that'. He'll tell you to go
along *the motorway*, thinking that only a fool wouldn't
know that he is referring to the M1, M4, M6, M62 or
whichever it happens to be.

Granted, some idiots take a risk by trying to pull people's
legs about local directions. It is done in various ways. 'See
that block of flats there and the bridge near that crossroads

behind them? Well, it's not that way but the other . . . .' or
'How do you get to Camden Town?', and then, after the
route has been explained at great length, 'Do you really? I go
this other way . . .' But in other cases seemingly idiotic
directions are well meant. People will thoughtlessly refer, say,
to Jesson's Garage, which hasn't existed for fifteen years, and
sometimes be understood. They still seem to see it there and
don't believe it has gone.

Nor should we forget that proverbial sayings include the
direction-finding variety. Of a long-winded person, for instance, Shropshire workers will say, 'He's going all round the
Wrekin', a type paralelled by similar sayings from other parts
of England. But, here, at least, though the criticised speaker's
language may be unclear, there is no doubt what his work-
mates mean.

Folklore also has a disturbing effect on industrial language
and the ideas it conveys. Here we are thinking not so much of
ancient legends, which, through being handed on verbally so
many times, become less and less authentic; but of modern
beliefs, customs and sayings. Many old fishermen believe that
people are born on the flowing tide and die from natural
causes on the ebb, that the weather will improve as soon as
the tide turns, that (impressed by the 'magic' number) every
seventh wave is exceptionally big or has the devil in it, or that
'When the wind is in the south, it blows the bait out of the
fish's mouth'.

The last reminds us that, despite daily T.V. and radio
weather forecasts, many people rely more on their own
weather sayings, such as: 'Rain before 7, fine before 11'; 'If
Candlemas Day be fair and clear/There'll be two winters in
the year'; 'A rainbow at night is a shepherd's delight'; 'If the
cock goes crowing to bed/He'll certainly rise with a watery
head'. Older folk sometimes talk of an exceptionally fine day
as a *weather breeder*, meaning that it will be followed by a
spell of bad weather. Such sayings of doubtful truth we tend
to forget when they go wrong, but we pride ourselves about
them when they come right. You can hear it said, 'When the
day lengthens, cold strengthens'; or of a blustery day, 'It's
enough to blow t'nebs (bills) off t'geese!' Some folklore may
be quite sensible, but really, if you were to believe it all, logic

and meaningful language as we know them would be no
more.

Curious and amusing though such beliefs may superficially
be, the superstitious ignorance they betray shows a sad
poverty of life. Some women say and believe: 'the sun turns
yer brains', 'earwigs crawl through yer brains to yer ears'; or
on moving from one council house to another persuade their
children to take bugs from the old house with them in
matchboxes for luck, or continue the old practice of 'sewing
their children in' for the winter (done in Cornwall within the
last fifteen years). Such horrors should be no delight of a
linguist or folklorist – they are urgent problems for the
sociologist to work on.

It is noteworthy that a modern industry like mechanical
engineering harbours very few superstitions. If a mechanic
grumbles that the *gremlins* have been at work, he has no
fairy-tale belief in those mischievous sprites. When a nut
won't go on and he grumbles that it's a case of *Sodd's Law*
(by which, however many you try, none will fit), he doesn't
really believe that someone discovered and teaches that law.
Car-sprayers drink plenty of milk and know why it is
recommended. Battery-makers have a hazardous job, dealing
with lead and needing special ventilation, and with creams
and eyewash always available. They go for regular check-ups,
where doctors assess their lead count. You are unlikely to
find dangerous modern industries hindered by foolish superstition and quack remedies.

The question after all this naturally arises, 'How far is
occupational language overheard in a pub, for example,
intelligible to a stranger?' It should be fairly understandable
unless the talk concentrates on work, when the stranger may
be baffled by the apparent vagueness of some terms and the
precise technicality of others. For instance, if it is miners
who are speaking, he may catch just the general word
machine for a particular coal-getting machine; but then hear
others far too exact for him, like *crawley* for a steel
conveyor, *shearer* and *trepanner* for types of coal-cutters,
panzer and A.M.C.O. for types of loaders, *sigh-grove* for a
new system of intercommunication or *dosco* for a special
machine for advancing a heading or roadway. Electrical

engineering is a very different industry linguistically, because its ordinary workers are at least semi-skilled and so their English ought to be reasonably understandable to anyone. Their industry does indeed have few dialectal terms; but again, because of its copious slang, abbreviations and technical jargon, it can be well-nigh unintelligible to a stranger.

Of course, there is no special reason why occupational language should be toned down for a casual listener's benefit: it is for communication between specialists for their mutual benefit alone. It can't really be equated with the golfer who shouts 'Fore! and expects the absent-minded walker straying near the green to know what he is raving about. Far better to yell 'Watch out!', though it is a word longer, or 'Ger off, you stupid —', and then the unfortunate fellow will rapidly sense the danger, from ball or player.

We mustn't, however, fall into the common trap of overdramatising communication barriers amongst speakers of different types of language. Internationally, language troubles have been blamed for riots in Pakistan and Ceylon, and troubles in countries like Czechoslovakia and South Africa, when the root causes are rather economic and political. If Switzerland can peacefully harbour four languages, besides the many dialects of its cantons, there seems no reason why British factory workers, though speaking rather differently from each other and very differently from most management, shouldn't pull together, provided working conditions are sound and industrial goals understood.

Rochdale textile operatives have a saying, 'I corn't keep t'bant on t'nick', literally 'I can't keep the twine on the groove', for the rare occasions when they a have a fellow-worker with whom they just can't get on. There is no reason for this situation to grow — at least no language reason, provided we are tolerant with a friend's odd sayings. If he repeats till you are tired of it 'I mean to say' or 'Eh?', please don't clobber him over the head just for that — perhaps he can't help it. Many obstacles remain to understanding language throughout industry, but very few are insurmountable.

15 Unscripted Narrations and Conversations

To show that this book is not based on a theoretical reconstruction of some non-existent or almost obsolete industrial language, tape-recordings of various speakers have been made. In some ways they show far more eloquently than separate chapters on different aspects, what actually happens to living language. From them stand out all the layers of language common to any speaker. The tape-recordings were transcribed phonetically, along with stresses and intonation patterns, though for present purposes they have been put into normal spelling. Probably the most notable feature of the first two extracts is the amount of deviation from exact occupational language, a deviation almost always towards Standard English.

EXTRACT 1

This is from a conversation between an old inshore fisherman (R.S.) of eighty-eight and a retired ferry-skipper (W.W.) of sixty-five. The older man did nearly all the talking. His voice was strong, and the unconcerned way he spoke for half an hour without sign of tiring was remarkable. Indeed, the following day he insisted on singing into the microphone a sea-chanty of some twenty-five verses, although this contained too much repetition and standard idiom to make dubbing on to discs worth while.

'Light-moon flood, and the mate took the dark-moon ebb. I'd — I'd a good experience o' that.'
'Oh, it were . . .'
'Blackest watch o' the lot.'
'There's none of 'em cared about the dark-moon ebb, but they all liked the light-moon.'
'Oh, aye. Oh, I know we — we had a do once in the — er — in the *Desdemonia*. Old John Nuttal was — you knowed Old John?'

'Oh, yes, I noo him.'

'Well, we were running down from — we were running along Laxey — er — past Laxey, making fer Ramsey Bay, an' it were blowing hard an' we'd two reeves* in, and Old John happened to put his tiller a little bit o' one side an' over the mainsail came, broke all the reef-ear-rings,† an' then we'd full sail on. Then we had to down with all the lot of it on deck until we got our reef-ear-rings made all right. We once — once in — in — er — in Laxey Bay there, we once picked a little lad up i' t' net.'

'Aye?'

'Aye! An, we had a do at Peel one time in these nick — er — they call 'em nickies,‡ don't they?'

'Yis.'

'Two masts, going a-herring fishing. One of 'em, he couldn't get in, he didn't know where he was, an' we went to his rescue an' fetched him in. . . . On a Saturday night, when we come in from sea, Church Street used to be our place, silk velvet wesket on, blue Devon jackets an' weskets, an' a velvet collar on your jacket, and there we used to stand, discussin' where the best place was for fishin'. Women used to ask their husbands, "Where have you been?" "Oh, I've been i' th'Ole" or "I've been on t'Showd" or "I've been on t'Slaughter" § On t'Slaughter we — er — used to go for — er — ray, plenty of good ray, an' in the 'Ole we used to get cod, an' on t'Showd we used to get plaice-flukes an' gurnets¶ and that. But we used to have to sort it out. Yellow gurnets an' plaice went as prime, grey gurnets went as offals, they didn't — only — er — so many a basket. Yellow gurnets an' plaice were sold so much a score, in weight, but ray an' that were sold by so much a basket, so was grey gurnets, so was dogfish.'

---

*Horizontal portions of a sail which may be folded.
†Rings in a sail, used for attaching a rope to fold the sail. A term unrecorded in OED or EDD.
‡Two-masted Manx herring-drifters.
§ Names of fishing grounds in the Irish Sea.
¶ Gurnards.

'Aye.'

'Oysters were sold at . . .'

'They counted 'em.'

'. . . at — er — seven an' six a hundred. Seven an' six a hundred fer — fer — er — oysters, but you used to have to give good count, one to every quarter. There were four oysters over the hundred every time, an' little oysters, well, they were kept in a bag separate. Them was — er — always divided between the crew, er — that would be stocker.'*

'They used to drag fish up into t' — from the boat to the warehouse.'

'Oh?'

'The men was called maggies.'

'Oh, aye. They once — they once fetched a porpoise-pig in, an' they had it down there — they had it down side o' t' fish warehouse. There were sixpence a time to have a look at a whale, they'd caught a young whale, an' it were sixpence a time, an' there were scores of people come. "Come on! Lood at this here — er — young whale we've got." Fancy! Sixpence apiece!'

EXTRACT 2

This is part of an explanation by a carpenter (T. B., aged sixty) to a layman of some of his trade terms. Besides its technical language, it is notable for all the mistakes, hesitations, repetitions and speech-fillers so typical of much talk by nearly all of us in casual conversation:

Fixers are outside workers. Then you get bench hands — that's the two distinctions, see? Go through the papers, you'll see 'bench hands wanted' or 'fixers wanted' or sometimes they'll advertise 'first fixers wanted', 'second fixers', 'final and finishing fixers'. It is more or less modern terms because, you see, there's so much piece-work and bonus work — you see the work is more or less subdivided — well, what they term in — er — they get joists — fixing joists — ground, you know — ground-floor chamber

---

*See *OED stocker*, sb., 5.

joists or they get roofing — they get roofing hands, you
know — putting the roof on, and then from them they get
what we term as fillers' fixing — that is, all — everything up
to plastering, see? Your floors, stairs, windows, all — see
that all the windows are in — are fixed — if they need any
fixing — door-casing. I mean a bricklayer only — he only
sort of props 'em in and he might — sometimes he builds a
head in if they have joggles on — those are the bits that
lean on the door heads or windows. . . . The mid-feather is
the brickwork dividing between the two flues — you see
you get two brick flues as you come up if you, say, you've
a fireplace up — upstairs, you come up here with this flue
and then you gather over to one side of your upstairs
fireplace like, coming up here, and then you come up with
your flue from your upstairs fireplace like, coming up
here, and then you come with your flue from your upstairs
fire and eventually — er — I mean, you can't come too
sharp but you gather them together and take them up in
one, you see, with just a four-and-a-half — er — you
know — width of a breadth between them — that's why
you get troubles in — in — stacks, where you get smoke in
your bedrooms where you've got — er — a brick out in the
mid-feather.
    . . . During the war I was working in Trafford Park
or — well, it is Cubitts — was then Holland, Hannen and
Cubitts of London — in fact it was at Hedley's soap works,
Procter and Gamble, and we was doing an extension there.
I've been mainly on housing, but I had to laugh at
this — er — at this Cockney — he was a joiner — he come
out o' Limehouse . . .'

EXTRACT 3

This is part of a conversation between two West Riding farm
labourers, R.M. and A.M., in their fifties. It is much more
consistently dialectal than the other extracts, and quite racy,
doubtless because farming has been one of the occupations
least affected by Standard English:

   'Hello, Alf. Wheer ta for? Off a bit? I see thou'rt dolled
   up.'

'Nay, not far, I'm just walkin' out a bit, that's all. Tha sees I'm out o' work ageean.'

'Out of work, arta? By gow, thou'rt about as well off as me, and tha knows they say theer's nobbut a awpny* i't'week between t'worker and t'laiker† at t'year end and t'laiker 'es it. If thou'rt to aks me, 'ere I am tewin' away t'week long for next to nowt, just keepin' body an' soul together an' niver an openin' for nowt. I were just grummlin' to misen for there's bahn' to be a do down at t'Wheeatsheeaf within the next week — tha'll 'av heerd on it, I expect?'

'No, I 'edn't.'

' 'esn't ta?'

'No.'

'Aye, an' I sud‡ like to gooa bur a'v nooa brass. I daresay they'd let me in baht payin' but I don't like to be beholden to folk. I tell thi what a'v been thinkin' o' doin', but tha mun niver mention it while breeath draws up an' down thi. I were thinkin' of offerin' to do my share i' potayts. Jack Hollins has a grand lot at t'back o' t'hedge, he'd never miss a rooit§ or two.'

'Tha wodn't call it reight steylin', Dick, wud ta?'

'It just depends, tha sees. If we just took an odd rooit here an' there and just thinned 'em out a bit and so gev t'others a better chance to grow an' spreyd, Jack would have as many potayts together as if we'd never touched 'em. We should be takkin' them an' that's steylin' in a way o' speykin', but if we could do Jack a good turn we mud as weel do it.'

'I'd rayther say nowt about it. I don't think Jack likes me.'

'Doesn't ta? Aw reight, then, we'll just ger 'em an' eyt 'em an' let that fit us for this time. We can do Jack a good turn some time else. An' if t'potayts is poor 'uns, we couldn't speyk a good word for 'em.'

'We'd better say nowt about 'em.'

---

*Halfpenny.
†Person off work.
‡Should.
§Root.

16 General Conclusions

Are we heading, however, towards a time when spoken and written language will no longer exist? It is certainly beginning to look like it, judging by the ever-increasing rash of symbols in traffic signs, scientific equations and so on.

The earliest writing represented objects by pictures — for the idea of a leg, you drew a leg. Then the drawing of a leg began to convey the idea of something more than 'leg', the concept of walking. Later, symbols could stand for sounds as well as ideas, as nowadays in musical notation.

Long ago, with the invention of alphabets, it became possible to communicate in writing without symbols; yet in some ways modern civilisation seems to be regressing. Every twenty miles or so along the motorway we are greeted by a colourful but childish-looking set of pictures — a petrol pump, capital P for parking, cup, fork and knife (in that order of priority?) — as if we couldn't recognise, looming well ahead, a motorway restaurant and service station. This doesn't mean that we have ever quite lost the use of symbols in written language. We use @, p., &, %, +, = and so forth on the typewriter and in manuscript, and this is no very new feature; but nowadays we rely increasingly on signs — the traffic warden's *lollipop* sign, yellow lines and criss-crossings on the roads, childlike drawings of men and women over public convenience entrances, traffic signs meaning 'pass either side', 'no stopping', 'no entry' etc., and chemical equations like

$$x = \frac{\Pi\sqrt{r^2 + z}}{2(z - 1)} \, ,$$

which would be so difficult and take so long to express verbally.

Professor Marshall McLuhan is quite dogmatic about the need for short-cutting words in one industry, electronics. He thinks that the purpose of electricity is the impulse carrying the message, which needs no words. His prophecy is frightening in its portayal of a languageless, completely computerised existence:

> Electric technology does not need words any more than the digital computer needs numbers. Electricity points the way to an extension of the process of consciousness itself, on a world scale, and without any verbalization whatever. The computer, in short, promises by technology a Pentecostal condition of universal understanding and unity. The next logical step would seem to be . . . to by-pass languages in favour of a general cosmic consciousness . . . paralleled by the condition of speechlessness that could confer a perpetuity of collective harmony and peace.

But this is an American view of one industry and, fortunately one might say, of a time still remote — Marshall McLuhan still has to convey his sense (or nonsense?) through words. All credit to him for letting us see some of the possibilities; but, if the day ever comes when Britishers are scientifically gagged like this, many will surely throw themselves under the nearest bus. Indeed, in direct contrast to what Marshall McLuhan claims, scientific language is actually expanding, and people with limited vocabulary are thought second-class citizens.

Let's move to a happier and more practical consideration, for occupational speech is never going to die, and so we just have to go on using and understanding it. Some levelling takes place, of course, but levelling and decay of occupational dialects have been slow, for, as fast as one occupation becomes extinct, another with its new and growing terminology is born. Most workers won't try to *scrape their tongue* (refine their speech) even if the doctor or the vicar calls or the boss appears on a tour of inspection; so that speech which is unorthodox but typical of the various occupations is widespread at home, more still in pubs and clubs, and naturally strongest of all at work.

Some dismal Johnnies will bemoan anything. Way back in 1899 Joseph Wright, perhaps the greatest dialect expert ever, lamented that local dialects were rapidly disappearing. Well, we know from acquaintances who utter outlandish expressions like the North-Eastern *az gannen yam* (I'm going home)

or the South-Western *'er'll give it to 'e* (She'll give it to him)
that the old regional dialects are far from dead. Most are still
vigorous, though it is only to be expected that gradually
those of remote hamlets will lose their special features and
we shall be left with regional dialects of larger areas, particularly the great conurbations like London, Glasgow, Birmingham, Liverpool, Leeds and Manchester. Thus, even local
dialect will remain for a long time.

When we consider occupational dialects, survival into the
foreseeable future is a certainty. With their mixtures of local
speech, slang, abbreviations, vulgar language and technical
jargon, they are too indigestible mouthfuls for Standard
English to swallow. If they were dying, the great interest they
arouse and the miniature civilisations they describe would
make them well worth saving. But occupational dialects are
no museum pieces. The Celtic languages of Old Cornish and
Manx have died out simply because there is no one left to
speak them. This fate can never befall industrial language, for
no one can imagine Britain without industry. The language in
all its variations is strongly alive, crying out for serious study
by the scholar and competent use by all in industry. Forget
the grammarians, elocution teachers and 'refaned' B.B.C.
pundits; and when in industry speak as its more sensible
speakers do.

Whether occupational speech should stay exactly as it is
poses another and an important question. It still seems that
industrial workers' efforts to express themselves are far from
perfect. It would be foolish to mock those efforts, to smile at
their curious pronunciations, word choice and grammar.
Many are men who have had the minimum legal period of
education, and since then may have had precious little call to
use even that. Many have had to go to work as soon as they
could to support their families. If they had had the educational opportunities of some modern, pampered layabouts,
they would have made startling and deserved progress up the
social and financial scales.

Somewhere, however, in their minds their lack of formal
education troubles them. This shows itself most at committee
meetings, where they are constrained by ignorance of procedure. Although committee procedure, which has grown up

through the years, is designed to give a fair crack of the whip to everyone, it can, under an inefficient chairman, make them feel uncomfortable. Faced with minutes, motions, amendments, attempted amendments to amendments, and points of order, their creative ideas can be left ashamedly unexpressed; and this is a pity for, when anyone has something worth saying, people will listen.

When some workpeople do try to speak in the official tongue, the saddening thing about their gibberish is not its illiteracy; on the contrary, it is its desperate striving after what they imagine to be educated talk: 'in order which', 'in which he was not in agreement with', 'different to this here motion', 'they saw he and I'.

There seems to be a tendency for those who have not had, or have not benefited from, formal education to try to deck out their speech, their thought, with the trappings of what they imagine to be the speech and thought of their intellectual betters. Those betters are, of course, mythical, but that in itself would not matter; in their attempt to imitate them, the imitators only demonstrate their inability to do so, and that does matter, since it exposes them to ridicule or pity; but what matters most is the increasing polarisation of society between educated articulateness on the one hand, and gruesomely illiterate incoherence on the other. Remember that, in works councils and management—worker meetings, millions of pounds and the personal and working lives of thousands of people can be at stake, so it is important to get facts and understanding right and to foster worthwhile initiative. Using a mess of words that one does not understand has the opposite effect — it confuses listeners and speaker, blurs his individuality into dull uniformity, gets him nowhere, and is no use to the committee and the section of society it represents.

Impressive differences often appear between artificial and natural language. A speaker will monotonously deliver a set talk but afterwards, answering questions off guard, he will reply directly, sincerely and effectively. Often, when strikers' wives are being interviewed on T.V., they will make no attempt to apply their husbands' unsteadily deployed and lifeless union jargon, but will speak their minds in words that come up fresh and hot. They have not erected a barrier between their thoughts and their speech as their husbands have.

Why does anyone believe that he ought to speak better than he can, and so in the end speak far worse than he might? Partly because silly people who imagine themselves superior to him have encouraged him in the belief; but mostly because the 'education' he gets can often be the mechanical application of old imperfect spelling, grammatical and stylistic instructions.

Britishers today who left school at the age of fifteen may not be so much better equipped than their grandparents who left full-time schooling at ten. Many are half-educated, taught enough to know that there is good in possessing words and the ability to use them, but not taught enough to allow them actually to have at their command sufficient words to sound or write as they think they should. But the half-educated, in that case, have been abominably cheated; for the wholly educated can sound as they please, and the uneducated can sound natural. Only many of the workpeople in the middle have virtually lost the power of accurate expression. An education which teaches its pupils to read and write without indicating *what* they ought to read and write, and without showing why they are being taught it, seems to have gone sadly wrong.

But, where great language gulfs remain, there should be more attempts to accept within reason the other fellow's mode of speech. A slice of bad language from a foreman to an operative should not be allowed to grow into a major dispute, nor should a factory-floor argument over who does what paralyse through lack of conciliatory efforts a whole industry. We don't want in industry a form of continuing civil war in which every Britisher would be the victim. To be a well-intentioned and sympathetic conciliator or arbitrator is not enough: one must understand the language of both sides of industry to appreciate their true hopes and intentions.

Forget, therefore, extreme arguments like Marshall McLuhan's about language disappearing, about something that will never happen. Nor should it go: there is too much work for it in conversation, explanations, instructions and peace-keeping. Let us stick to realities, grapple with the big communications problems that do exist, particularly in large firms, and say as clearly and as tactfully as possible whatever seems needed. Then, whether it approaches Standard English or not, our occupational language will best fulfil its vital purpose.

Part E   Selected Industries

17 Household Words

Domestic matters not only affect us all, but linguistically should be most significant. Farming and mining have some of the oldest words because they are among the oldest industries, and by the same reasoning housekeeping will prove a very rewarding subject. To analyse only men's industries would be grossly unfair, so let us start this survey of some particular industries by trying to redress the balance.

We often forget that the housewife is a specialised worker. She has cooking skills, mending skills, cleaning and child-coaxing skills; terms like *non-stick pans* mean a lot to her. 'Industrial' action now goes well beyond older spheres — teachers and civil servants, for instance, consider taking it — and in the context of labour relations it embraces all kinds of work. Even though housewives haven't yet gone on strike, they are unrecognised industrial workers.

The degrading image of the housewife wearing *kegs* or hair-curlers all day long and ineffectually trying to quieten a pack of screaming *kids*, does her scant justice. She has to be ideally a skilled communicator because of the pressures that may be brought to her at the door. Brush and insurance salesmen, Jehovah's Witnesses and so on make it a persuaders' paradise. It is fortunate, though, that she can retreat from it. How often do ladies say, 'I agree with you, but I've got something in the oven'!

It is interesting to see how near women's magazines come to the industrial language of the housewife, and which comes nearest. We know they offer the fantasy world, of course, but they also take care to cover the industrial aspects — dressmaking and fashion, knitting (*Woman's Weekly* boasts on its cover that it is 'famed for its knitting'), cooking, cleaning, child care and even marital problems. In the weeklies, although the stress given to different aspects varies in each paper from issue to issue, our survey found that *Woman's Realm* usually covers them best, followed closely by *Woman's Weekly*, although sometimes the week's best coverage is provided by *Woman's Own*. However, for the most comprehensive approach to such matters, one must turn to the dearer monthlies, especially *Good Housekeeping* and then *Ideal Homes*.

Let us start our house language investigation with house types. Scottish mining areas have their two-roomed *but-an-bens*, literally 'outside-and-withins', and many English old working-class districts their *back-to-backs* without back door, back garden or back yard. Some names are a little harder to understand. Even *detached houses* sound as if they have been once joined, whilst *semis* might more properly be named *three-quarters-detached*, since they have only one party wall. *Quasi-semis*, joined by their garages, certainly act as *semis*, though their Latin *quasi* sounds so foreign to English speech. *Town houses* turn out to be modern versions of terraced houses. But the prize for unusualness must go to *inverted houses* (builders' term) or, as they are popularly called, *upside-down houses*. These are no fairy-tale structures but sound dwellings built in parts of Sheffield and elsewhere, on steep hillsides on a Swiss pattern, with the bedrooms at the rear and downstairs.

Approaches to the house are puzzling. Streets are beginning to disappear, at least in name, to make way for tastefully-named *avenues, closes, folds* and so on. In many places the narrow passage between houses is the *snicket*, originally it seems a name for a simple form of latch on a gate, then for the gate itself, and eventually for the footpath or alley which the gate closed. But it assumes many aliases — to name a few, *jinnel, ginnel, gunnel, troughing, tewer, smoot*, in part of Cheshire the remarkable *giggle-gaggle* and in Cornwall sometimes *dranjey*. The *wint* is different. This is an alleyway with rooms above it bisecting a pair of *semis*, and no doubt deriving its name from the wind that draughtily blows through it.

Rooms have always had special names. The most chameleon-like one has been the comfortable one downstairs where you would entertain an important visitor. Once it was the *drawing-* (from *withdrawing-*) *room* because the ladies retired to it for conversation after dinner. Then, with the same underlying meaning, it became the *parlour* (from

French *parler*, 'to speak'), then *best room, front room* or *sitting-room*. Some Yorkshire housewives call it just *t'room*, as if it is the only part of the house worth calling a room! Now, however, it is usually the *lounge* or, combined with living-room, a *through-lounge*.

Country mansions have supplied many humbler dwellings with a *hall* (for earlier *vestibule*) and *pantry* (from the butler's pantry); but the *scullery* or *backhouse* (back kitchen) tends to resist a more elegant name. The *chamber* or *chaumer* has become a bedroom; the *netty, nessy* (from *necessary*), *dunnekin* or *privy* has become, through euphemism and/or slang, a *W.C., lavatory, toilet, cloakroom* (without hat-pegs), *smallest room* or *loo* (apparently from *Waterloo*); whilst new or new-sounding extensions like *car-ports, sun-lounges* and *patios* keep appearing. If you live in a *sunshine semi* boasting smart appendages like these, you can feel justly proud.

Antiquated yard brushes, brooms and *besoms* have given way to Hoovers and the like. Much apparatus associated with the old-fashioned fireplace has gone. Gone are *ass-'oles* under the fire for the ashes to drop into, *bellowses, draw-tins,* and most of the *fire-potters* or *fire-points* (pokers). Coal-scuttles or *skeps*, shovels or *shools*, tongs and *cow-rake* are rare; and *inglenooks* almost extinct. Many a housewife, remembering the Friday chores of black-leading the old-fashioned hearth, has been delighted to exchange it for the luxuries of central heating.

Untidy housewives abound, judging by all the so-called *slatterns, trolly-mogs, slovens* and *tosspots* whose houses are a *proper sipperty*, i.e. a complete mess. Also there seems to be an incredible number of gossips, busybodies or *Nosey Parkers* with their *curtain-pimping* ('-peeping'); and a host of *clat-cans* and *toots* with all their *calling, camping* (without tents) and *tooting,** i.e. gossiping ('She were round 'ere tootin' again this morning'). But don't be alarmed: all these names arise because such people, though a small minority, incite pointed comment in all cultures.

An English family's home being its castle, people as well as things are naturally thought of from that viewpoint. This is

*With its interesting etymology from Anglo-Saxon *tōtian* 'to espy'.

why *our* is such a distinguishing feature of much family speech, where it is almost essential in discussing a relative (*our Jack's wife, our Molly*, etc.). So much was this once the case that in some families it was a form of address. Sisters would say to brothers, 'Gi' us a bit, our Joe', and children would address their mother as *our Mum*. Its utility today is shown especially in large families where the family's Jack or Molly has to be distinguished from other people's Jacks and Mollies. It has nicer ramifications, as when you start referring to *their Molly*, which always sounds rather disparaging.

Services to the house and the men operating them have changed. *Cannels* and oil-lamps have given way to *the lektrik*. No longer can you hear drivers of horse-drawn wagons laden with grimy bulging bags shouting 'Coal! Coal! Shillin' 'undredweight', and more modern coalmen with their *nutty slack* etc. are decreasing in numbers. The humble *rat*-catcher has become euphemistically a *rodent inspector*, and similarly *the man from t' Watter Board* appears as a *sanitary inspector* or *water department official*; whilst in parts even the postman is changing, to the *delivery officer*.

In small communities there is still much contact with tradesmen at the door, but there can be little in skyscraper flats. Broadly, we seem to be in a transitional period between the time when the housewife's ears were assailed by incessant street-cries, and the increasingly abstract world of shopping in discount store and hypermarket.

Apparatus and furniture have changed immensely in type, appearance or at least name. Prams or babies' cradles may be *bassinets*; food cupboards may be *hutches* or *ambries*; chests may still be *kists*; stools can be *crackets, crickets, creepers* or *creepies*; buffets can be *Humpties* (cf. Humpty Dumpty), *puffies* in Cheshire, *tuffets* (Anglesey) or *puffles* (Cornwall). And, even with modern furniture, problems lie unsolved. Why, for instance, do we talk of *a bunk bed* when we mean two of them? However, in the brave new indoor world of *vacs, mixers, mincers* and all the rest, such tiresome language details are conveniently forgotten.

In the terraced-house districts an important status symbol used to be the *sheffoneer*. The more elaborate its columns, mirrors and so on, the higher was its status; its cherished, highly polished surface was usually protected by lace mats on which stood a bewildering collection of *whim-whams* in cheap pot and glass, photos, sea-shells, artificial flowers and any other objects which would reflect credit on the household. The *cornish* above the parlour fireplace would carry the same type of decoration, and that room might have an aspidistra and be equipped so that the family could boast 'Our Martha's lernin' t'pianer'. Now, of course, around the house very different things are the focus of pride and enjoyment — a *transistor* perhaps (instead of the old-fashioned *wireless*), car, boat, caravan, *fridge*, cassette or colour *telly*. Or the boast may be, 'We've got stereo'.

Now and then there crop up round the house surprisingly old-fashioned clothing words. *Clouts* for clothes (like *clout* for a dishcloth) is still sometimes found; as are *shift* or *shimmy* for chemise (the last through taking *chemise* as a plural), and *pilch, hippin, double* or again just *clout* for nappy. Some men of the house say *muffler* for scarf, *breeches* for trousers and *coat* for jacket, though most people maintain that the last pair are quite different and always have been.

Old habits and traditions don't die but either modulate in a changed society or become masked by a false front. Examples are very noticeable in the relaxed area of the home, where the continuity of life is most protected, and nowhere has this been more so than on washing day.

A *peggy* (called also *dolly-peg* or *maiden*) was used for turning the clothes in the *keeler* or *dolly-tub*. Water was baled with a *piggin* or *lading can*. The housewife would *sind* instead of rinse the clothes. To take them out to dry, she would carry them in a *voider* or clothes-basket, but, if it rained and she wanted to dry them before the fire, she would hang them on the *maiden* ('clothes-horse') or *winteredge*. This last derives from before the Industrial Revolution, when during the dry summer months clothes would be spread outside on hedges but in winter hung inside on a wooden frame — hence very logically a *winter-hedge*, from which over the years the *h* has disappeared. In this era of coin-in-the-slot laundrettes, tumble-driers and twin-tub washers one would imagine such words extinct, but pensioners know them quite

well. Similarly with *possing* in the *posser*: one might think
that the words had died with the *possers* themselves, some of
them rather splendid copper affairs. But doubtless somewhere in England at this moment a woman who has switched
on her automatic washing-machine is telling a neighbour, 'I've
just put the clothes in to poss'.

Food, like household life generally, is rather a neglected
subject, historically speaking; yet the kitchen, so central to
the running of a house, has provided many interesting and
important terms. Out of it once came great and glorious
dishes like simnel cake for Mothering Sunday, Spotted Dick,
broth and dumplings, homemade sly cake, pig's cheek, tripe,
crab salad. . . . What we have lost in the modern rush of life!

Food in general has many local, occupational and slang
names. A person feeling unwell may be off his *feed* (like an
animal), *meat* (dialectal), *grub, peck, snap* or *tommy* (the last
two being originally miners' words).

Through shop influence, names for kitchen apparatus and
utensils are becoming more standardised. Thus *oons* and
yubbens have been normalised to ovens, *thibles* to porridge
sticks, and *possnets* to saucepans. But kitchen processes and
descriptions can still bewilder. To get the boiling water from
kettle to teapot, most people pour it, but others, like
steelmen with molten metal, *teem* it, using an old Anglo-
Saxon word (*tāeman*). Some of us quite normally make a cup
of tea; but millions of others *mek, mak, brew, mash, scald,
soak, wet* or even *turn* it. Some people thicken gravy whilst
others *lithen* it; in some homes unrisen bread is *sad*, and
bacon with a strong nasty taste is not rancid but *reasty*.

Kitchen delicacies provide many emotive names. There are
girdle cakes known as *spice fizzers* or in Northmberland
singing hinnies; fat rascals (rich teacakes); *maidens' honours*
(the almond-topped rich cakes surmounted by a cross); *love
cakes* (raspberry sandwiches); *church windows*, most descrip-
tively for Battenberg or mosaic cakes, with alternate squares
of pink and yellow. *Orts* (possibly from *aughts*) are crumbs
or leavings of any description. Even common food ingredients can retain very different older names, like *alicker* for
vinegar (literally from French for 'ale-sour'), *barm* throughout Lancashire for yeast, *sawt* for salt, and *saim* for lard.

The teacake question is quite involved. In Sheffield, for example, the plain variety is a *bread-cake* as opposed to the currant one, which is just a *teacake*; whereas in Leeds, Bolton and Manchester the plain ones are *flat-cakes* or *teacakes* and the others *currant teacakes*. Those who travel round a good deal often find it hard to remember which shop calls them which. There are other problems too. Are *pikelets* the same as *crampits* or *crumpits*; are *barm-cakes* muffins; and, if treacle is treacle and syrup is syrup, what is *black treacle*?

Interest in food and food words never flags. True, most people who hear an elderly housewife referring to *bought bread* think she is living in the past, thinking of the time when it had a homemade rival. But new eating words keep being coined, especially by the younger generation, such as *chuddy* for chewing-gum and *conny-onny-butties** for tins of condensed milk.

Although, sadly, some exciting dishes have gone, many remain to tickle the palate of the British workman, who keenly attacks menus like these:

Breakfast
    cornflakes
    fried bread, egg and bacon
lodging-house butty (alternatively *tramstopper* or *door-stopper*, a very thick one)
mug of tea
Snap or politely *Elevenses*   (about 10 a.m.)
    Irish boiled ham (i.e. cheese barm-cakes from the works canteen)
    can of tea
Dinner (mid-day)
    if at home, hot-pot, scouse, *bangers* (sausages) and mash, or pig's foot; followed by rice pudding or rolypoly, and tea
Knife and Fork Tea
    elder (boiled udder), jam or treacle butties, pie, parkin, and the inevitable tea

---

*Abbreviation + reduplication + dialect.

Evening Sustenance (about 9—10 p.m.)

   a *pint* (liquid unspecified and quantity most variable)
   sunk in the local pub

Late Supper (11 p.m.)

   fish, chips and peas, preferably eaten in the street on
   returning from the *chippy* or *fish-oil* (fish-and-chip
   shop) and out of a greasy paper bag, which supposedly
   enriches their taste: if at home, supplemented by *shives*
   of bread and, if he can manage it, more tea

Though space forbids detailed analysis, we should not
leave this section without at least touching upon a matter
vital to all households, namely affairs of the heart. *Courting*
is used, but seems a general polite word for a situation
involving several stages like *chatting her up, dating her*, being
on the arm or *walking her out, getting yer foot under t'mat*
and being *on a promise*, which leads to *getting wed* or *getting
spliced*. For 'living in sin', we find *living tally*, allegedly
linked with the miner's *tally* for his tub label; *living over the
brush*, apparently from gypsy weddings, where to show the
alliance one had publicly to jump over a brush; and the oddly
sanctimonious term *living Hallelujah*. Here, somewhat regret-
fully, we must halt domestic considerations to review
industries outside the house.

18 Coalmining Language

The material for this investigation was collected in visits from 1964 onwards to fifteen sections of the English, Scottish and Welsh coalfields (see map, p. 170). All were personally investigated, fourteen by me and the Scottish coalfield by Michael McMahon, linguistics lecturer at Jordanhill College of Education, who transcribed the speech of his Scottish miners with great phonetic accuracy. Interviews were often conducted in informants' own houses, where they could best relax; but also down the pit, in village halls and streets, and in a miners' hospital. Warm thanks are due not only to Mr McMahon for his willing assistance, but to National Coal Board publicity officers, union officials, colleagues who acted as contacts in the preliminary selection of helpers, pit managers and foremen, and above all to the informants themselves, for their patience and enthusiasm.

My interest in coalmining language had begun in the 1950s when I started in mid-term supply teaching in the West Riding. Miners could be recognised as those at village street corners sitting *on their hunkers* ('haunches', cf. *OED, hunkers*), and in school on non-formal occasions their children's vernacular was equally noticeable. It was astonishing, having laboured with an apparently normal secondary modern class most of the day, to supervise football or cricket matches where the pupils used a different language altogether. Just as puzzling, after a move to a Derbyshire grammar school in another mining district, was constantly to meet *thou* and *thee*, as in *Thou did it, Thee'll cop* ('catch') *it*. The latter usage, quite unlike Standard English and more typical of the West Country, does occur in parts of the Midlands.* Very salutary was the occasion when many of the pupils, told to collect and compare samples of native unorthodox grammar, returned with some prize specimens that had just issued from a fellow-teacher: after that I was

*See *EDD, thee*, II, 2.

1   AUCHINLOCK Dunb.
2   WHITBURN Durham
3   QUEENSBURY Yorks.
4   HOYLAND Yorks.
5   MALTBY Yorks.
6   WARSOP Notts.
7   CLIFTON Notts.
8   DEAL Kent
9   RADSTOCK Som.
10 EBBW VALE Mon.
11 CINDERFORD Gloucs.
12 COALBROOKDALE Salop.
13 WREXHAM Den.
14 PENDLETON Lancs.
15 MARYPORT Cum.

0   50   100
            Miles

Fig. 2 British coalfields

more careful. There were, too, remarkable meetings with audiences in mining communities, resulting in numerous questions (the attraction being not the speaker but the subject), where the response differed markedly from the polite acceptance similar talks might receive in, say, a residential city suburb.

In dealing with industrial speech, one also needs to take into account relevant historical and technical factors, which in mining are particularly daunting because miners have moved around a good deal. Right back in 1878, a report already stated that there had been 'frequent and large-scale exchange of miners and mining words between coalfields'.* Thus on the face of it there seemed slim hope of finding a pattern in British mining language. How far these fears were justified may be seen shortly.

At one extreme are a few very old collieries like place 12 on the map (the Shropshire collieries of Coalbrookdale were apparently shipping coal down the Severn in the seventeenth century). There are other survivors of larger colliery areas, like place 9, the Kilmerston pit at Radstock, the only one now working on the Somerset coalfield. The Whitburn pit (place 2) has closed, like all those in 'The Forest' (the Forest of Dean, including place 11). Linguistic problems certainly grow when, as so often, a pit draws many of its workers from other coalfields. For example, Cannock Chase, a deep-mining area which began in a big way about 1850, was manned chiefly from pits in Coalbrookdale and North Staffordshire which had closed; and more recently there have been big migrations from Country Durham to the Yorkshire–Derby-shire–Nottinghamshire coalfield, from the Forest of Dean to South Wales, and many forced moves from the Cumberland and Lancashire pits. The most acute linguistic problem occurs in the Kent coalfield, the youngest in the country and only sixty-six years old (mining started in 1908), because it has drawn some of its miners from the fishing industry and the great majority from all the other coalfields. One official who has worked for the last sixteen years at these mines insists that 'there is no Kent dialect', i.e. no local mining dialect,

* M. F. Wakelin (ed.), *Patterns in the Folk Speech of the British Isles*, p. 3.

there. Faced with all this, one can only listen to and question native miners from each area, and assemble the evidence to see what, if anything, it proves.

SELECTION OF RESULTS

The outstanding feature of our results is their variety, although they are far from haphazard. They bear little relation to Ellis's maps of local English areas;* but he was scrutinising general, not mining, language — and before 1890, which is a long time ago. From our recent survey, notions below are shown in capitals. Each is followed by local answers and bracketed numbers indicating from which of the fifteen investigated localities they came. * = unrecorded in *OED* and *EDD*.

1. MINE *mine* (11), elsewhere *pit*.
2. MINER *miner* (11, 12), *moiner* (9), *collier* (1, 3–5, 7, 15), *miner* + older *collier* (6, 13), *collier* if he works at the coal-face but otherwise *miner* (10), *cullier* + broader speech *pitman* (2), *pitman* (8).
3. DRIFT-MINE *duck** (1), *day-'ole* (2), *day-oil* (3), *day-'ole* + modern *foot-road* (4), *foot-road* (6), *day-'oil* + *drift* (5), *drift mine* (7), *foot-ridge* (12), *mine* if slanting down + *level* if entered horizontally (10), *level* (11, 13), *dee-eye* (14 — see *OED*, *day*, sb., 24).
4. STEEL BUCKET, once used for making a main shaft: *kettle* (1), *'opper* (3, 4, 11, 13), *'oppet* (6), *kibble* (5, 14), *skip* (9), *bowk* (12), *bowk* + *kep** (10).
5. PIT-HEAD *pet-hid* (1), *pet-head* (11, 12), *pit-top* (4, 6, 7, 8), *pit-head* + *pit-top* (10), *pit-top* + *pit-'eead* (3), *bank* (2), *pit-head* + pit-bank (13), *pit-top* + older *pit-bank* + technical *'eap-stead* (5), older *'eapstead* + more modern *pit-broo* (14).
6. SLAG HEAP *bing** (1), *(pit-)tip* (2–4, 6, 8, 10, 11), *pit-'ill* + *pit-tip* (5), *bonk* (14), *dirt-'eap* (7), *dirt-mount** (12), *spoil-bank* + *spoil'eap* + older *dirt-tip* (13), *tip* + older *batch* (9 — cf. *EDD bache*).
7. CHIEF PASSAGE IN MINE *main road* (1, 6, 10–12), *road* (7), *main roadway* (3), *main girder road* (15), *gate* + *roadway* + *plane* (5).
8. HAULAGE ROAD *causey** + *heading** (1), *jig* (12), jig + *rope road* (6), *ginny* (4, 5, 11), *incloin* (9), *incline* (10), *steep** (8), *break** (13), *spunney-broo** (spinney-brow) (14).

---

*I. A. J. Ellis *English Dialects: Their Sounds and Homes* (English Dialect Society, 1890).

9. SAFETY-HOLE, *man-hole* (1, 15), *refuge-'ole* (2), *man-'oil* + older *by-'oil* (3), *man-'ole* + *-'oil* (5), *man-'ole* (6, 8, 11, 12).

10. WIDENING THE ROADWAY *cheeking** + *brushing** (6), *cheeking* (5, 8), *back-brushing* (1, 15), *widdening* (4, 11).

11. SIDE ROAD *duck** + *heading* (1), *'eadin'* (10–12), *stall-gate* (6), *gate* (3, 5, 7, 8, 13), *turn-out* (9 — cf. *OED*, *turn-out*, sb., 4).

12. SMALL CONNECTING PASSAGE *througher** (1), *board* (3–5), *snicket* (6, 12), *slip-road* + near surface *snicket* (7), *snicket gate* (8), *stall-road* (10), *stall-road* + *up-cut** (11), *wind-road* (14), *cross-end** (15).

13. CUL-DE-SAC *blind heading* (1) — a term 'deprecated' by the British Standards Institution booklet no. 3618, *slip* (10), *stoppin'* (11), *fast-end* (5, 6, 7, 12).

14. MINER'S WORKING PLACE *oil* (3, e.g. 'That's Billy Puck's 'oil'), *stint* (7, 8, e.g. 'He's in 14 stint'), *place* (14), *place* + *stent* (1), *stall* (5, 6, 11, 12), *gannen-board* (2 — cf. *EDD*, *gan* v.[1], 3).

15. DEPUTY *deppaty* (2–4, 7, 12, 13), *fireman* + *deputy* (10), *shot firer* + *fireman* (1), *examiner* (9), *doggy** (14 — cf. *EDD*, *doggy*, sb.[1]), *debbaty* + *doggy* (5).

16. ONSETTER *onsetter* (2, 6–7, 11, 12, 14, 15), *'anger-on* (5), *'inger-on* (3), *'anger-on* + modern *onsetter* (4), *hitcher* (10), *on-setter* + more often *hitcher* (9), *pit-bottomer* (1), *hooker** (13).

17. CALLER *knocker-up* + *chapper-up** (1 — but cf. *chapper* 'door-knocker' under *EDD chap* v.[2]), elsewhere *knocker-up*.

18. PIT-CARPENTER *carpenter* (12), *shaftsman* (4, 6, 9, 14, 15), *ripper* (6, 10), *timberer** (5, 11), *joiner* (7), *janer* (1 — cf. under *EDD*, *joiner*, spelling *geinere*).

19. STALLMAN AND HIS HELPER *no words* (1), *collier* and *putter* (2), *collier* and *'urrier* (3), *stallman* and *trammer* (4), *stallman* and *butty* (5), *stallman* + older *butty* + *dayman* (6), *hewer* and *carting-boy* (9), *collier* and *butty* (10), *miner* and *butty* (11 — also as verb, to *butty* for someone), *collier* and *daytaler* (14).

20. COMPANIONS *nibbers** 'neighbours' (1), *marrers* (2, 15), else-where *mates*.

21. LUNCH *piece** (1 — cf. *EDD*, *piece-time*), *snap* in a *snap-tin* (4–7, 10, 12 14), *jock* in a *pit-'ankertch* (handkerchief) (3), *tommy* in a *tommy-box* (11), *bait* (2), *bait* + *crowdy* (15), *grub* in a *grub-tin* (9), *snap(pin')* (13).

22. STEP IN MINE FLOOR *throw** (3), *up-throw* (12), *canch** (6), *rise* (11), *trammin'-rise** (5), *jump-up* (7), *roll* + *canch* + *caunch* (13), *haytch** (1 — cf. *EDD*, *hatch*, sb.[4]), *bink* (15).

23. GRAIN IN COAL *slip* (9–11), *cleat* (6, 12, 15), *grain* (7), *grain* + *cleat* (13), *grain* + *teeth** (1), *cleat* + *shut** (14).

24. TO CUT UNDERNEATH COAL *hole* + *heowk* (1 — cf. *EDD*, *huck*, v.[3]), *hew* (2), *'ole* (5, 6, 11), *cut* (7, 10), *'ole* + *cut* (12, 13), *'ole* + *dint* (4), *hag* (15), *binch** (9).

25. SMALL CHOCK *geb* (see *EDD*, *jib*) + *stale** (1), *chock* (8, 11), *chocker** + *sprag* (6), *chock* + *sprag* (4), *sprag* + *clog* (5), *postin'** (3), *lid* + *head-tree* (15), *cog** (10).

26. WASTE AREA *gob-'oil* (3), *gob* (4–7, 9, 10, 12 14), *goaf* (2), *go-off* (15 — variant of last), *cundy* (1), *gob + waste* (11), *waste* (12, 13), *gob + goaf + waste* (8).

27. VERTICAL PROP *prop* (8, 11, 13, 14, 15), *long prop* (4), *prop + leg* (6, 7, 12), *leg* (1, 5), *arm* (10), *puncheon* (3), *post* under 3 ft. + *timber* over 3 ft. + *uproight + stimple* (9).

28. HORIZONTAL PROP *bar* (5, 6, 11–13), *bar + crown* (1), *punch(er)** (4), *collar* (10), *flat* (9).

29. WEDGE *wedge* (2, 13), *lid* (1, 3, 11, 12, 15), *gug** (9), *pad* (1 ft.) + *lid* (if 6 in.) (7), *cappin'* (14), *head-tree* (15).

30. PILLAR stoop + *pack* (1), *packin'* (6, 7), *pillar* of coal + *pack* of stones (14), elsewhere *pack*.

31. SLICE TAKEN OFF PILLAR *cut* (1, 13), *lift* (2), *jenk** (5), *jow* (14).

32. FILL IN CREVICES *gob in* (6), *stem* (1, 4, 12–15), *fill up* (3), *ram* (7, 9), *stem + ram* (11).

33. UPHEAVING OF FLOOR *hoving* (heaving) (1), *puff-up** (11), *puckin'* (10), *floor-lift** (4, 6, 7, 12–14), *floor-lift + floor-blow* (5, 8), *blow* (9).

34. DEPRESSION IN ROOF *slip* (3), *slip + pot-'ole* (6), *pot-'ole* (4, 5, 14), *stone* (2), *bad styan* (stone) (15), *bad 'ole* (7), *bad ground* (12), *bell* + welver** (11), *bell-mould* (9), *slip + swilly* (cf. *OED*, *swally*) + *roll* (13).

35. HOLLOW (adj., of coal) *boss* (1), *'oller* (3, 12, 14), *drummy** (5, 7), *drummy + 'oller + drawn* (6) *baggy* (4, 11, 15), *nesh* (13 – cf. *EDD*, *nesh*, adj., 2).

36. WATER CHANNEL *cutting* (1), *race + cutting + ricket* (5), *garland* (9, 13), *channel* (12, 13), *gully* (14). Note also *grip* at Wath-on-Dearne, West Riding Yorkshire.

37. TUB *hatch** (1), *chumman** for an empty one + *tub* (2), *corve* (3 – see *OED*, *corf*, 2b), *dram** (10, 11 – cf. *EDD*, *tram*, sb.,[1] 8), elsewhere *tub*.

38. *TUB FOR DEBRIS bogey* (1), *jotty** (5–7), *muck-tub* (4, 5), *dram** (10, 13), *dirt-tub* (13), *dirt-'oppet** (14), *supply-tub* (15), *dan* (12), *dilly* (9), *dobbin* (11).

39. TALLY ON TUB *tally* (9, 12, 13), *token* (1, 2, 15), *tally + cut* (14), *dommy** (3), 'only a number is chalked on' (7, 10).

40. TRAIN OF TUBS *reach** (1), *jag + tram* (4), *run + set* (6), *run* (7), *journey** (9, 10, 12, 13), *journey + jag* (11), *tub +* a small one *dram* (13), *gang* (14), *set + tram* (15).

41. BRAKE ON TUBS *snibble** (1), *cow* (2), *lashing-chain + clam-key* (4), *drag* (5), *clivvy* (clivvis) (6), *lounge* (9), *shackle* (10), *sprag* (11), *locker* (12, 13), *couplin'* (14), *breeak* (brake) (15).

42. COAL *coal + coa'* (1), *cwoal* (2), *coil* (3–5), *cooal* (9), *cwoll* (15), otherwise *coal*.

43. SMALL COAL *cobbles* (3, 5, 7, 10, 12), *smalls* (13, 14), *cobbles + smalls* (6), *nuts* (15), *smahl cwoal* (2), *duffy* (11 – see *EDD*, *duff*, sb.[2]).

44. COAL-DUST *coa'-dust* + *coom* (1), *duff* (2), *smudge* (4), *slack* (2, 6, 10–15), *sleck* (3, 5, 7), *gummin** (7).
45. POOR COAL 'very little poor coal' (1), *brockens** + *splents* (splints) (2), *bags* (4), *muck* (5), *motherin'** (9), *rashin'** (10), *clod* (11, 13), *rubbishy stuff* (12), *burgy* (14), *rubbish* (15).
46. CHALK-STONE *bindin'* (3, 11), *bind* (4, 5, 12), *bind* + *dirt-band* (6, 7).
47. GOLD-COLOURED VEIN *brass* (1, 2, 15), *brass lumps* (3), *brasses* (4), *connies** (5), *brassy coal* (6), *old coal* (7), *brahs* (10), *brassy** (11 – only as adj. in *EDD*), *brazzins** (12).
48. DEBRIS *dirt* (1, 7, 14), *dirt* + *muck* (13), *rip* + *lip** (8), elsewhere just *muck*.
49. DISCHARGE OF GAS *gobbin** (7), *gas* (9), *blower* (1, 4, 6, 9, 12, 15), *belch* (11).
50. VENTILATION SCREENS OR DOORS *air-doors* (4, 5, 12), *ventilation doors* (6, 9), permanent *doors* + temporary *brattices* (11), *brattice-cloths* (7), *braddish-cloths* (14), *braddish-doors* (15), *trap doors* (1), *watterproof sheets* (3), *'urdles* (5).
51. SCREENS FOR SORTING *tables* (1), *screens* (2–14), *screes* (15 – see *EDD*, *scree*, sb^2., 2).
52. SEDIMENT *slurry* (1), *muck* (4, 5), *sludge* (6, 11), *dirt* (7, 12), *billy** (10), *wash-muck* (15).
53. SORTER *check-weighman* (1–3, 8, 14, 15), *wagon-weighman* (2), *weigher* (10), *checker* (11, 12), *weigher* + *checker* (9), *sampler* (7), *clotcher** (4, 5).

From the mass above it is plain that for one notion a bewildering variety of answers may be obtained. This is because, just as in Standard English, each informant has several layers or registers of speech, all helping to blur any neat linguistic pattern, so that to make a completely accurate mining language map would require infinite detail. Thus the tub label was *tally* at Cannop but *motty* at Light Moor, pits only two miles apart in the Forest of Dean. In the West Riding, a ripper may be called *caunchman, dinter, (dummy-) brusher, fettler, kenchman, repairer* or *scourer*; and these terms are themselves rapidly changing with the nationalisation of the industry. For *stint*, the amount of work allotted to a miner, the West Riding has *stint* at Maltby, the curious and unrecorded *pog* at Kilnhurst and Denaby, and *sneck* (cf. *EDD*, *snack*, sb.^{1}) at Normanton – from pits within about a ten-mile radius. For *stallman*, the responses at Warsop gave first *chargeman*, next *stallman*, and finally the old word *butty* (cf. *EDD*, *butty*, sb.,^{1} 3). In Somerset, vertical wooden props were, according to the same Radstock informant, *posts* if under three feet, *timber* if longer, *uproights* in conversation with his friend and in broader dialect *stimples* (cf. *EDD, stemple*, unrecorded for Somerset and without an *i*-spelling) — in other words, four terms for a single basic idea. One might well wonder why the occupational dialect should make itself so complicated. Yet it happens too in the standard language, where for instance Old English *andwlīta* was apparently replaced by the French *face*, and where even today we have *bravery* alongside *courage*.

Sometimes it is impossible to equate answers because the whole idea is expressed differently. Thus, although a miner may often talk about being in a *team* (places 4, 11−14) and sometimes about his *gang* (4) or *pool* (1), he may have no corresponding word because he worked individually (6) or with one boy (3) or just says 'We work together' (7). For the direction of working, we confirmed that mines were thought of compasswise from the central shaft, but beyond this answers were difficult to compare. For example, 'I'm working down the north ducks' (1), 'I's working eighth high side' (2), 'I'm working on t'north side/west board/west ginny' (4), 'I'm working north/up west/down south' (6), 'I'm working B panel/I'm going A 10s' (7). Seeking local expressions for a roof collapse, I heard *fall* (4−7, 15); but also *There's bin a weight on*, i.e. a heavy fall (4), *It's weightin' a bit* (3) and *It's on weight* (11), i.e. 'It's ready to fall'.

Two extraordinary and so far unrecorded types of expressions have also been appearing. From the West Riding (place 3) comes *t'floor's fawn in* for 'the roof has collapsed'. But how can a roof be a floor? It seems nonsense to all but the speaker. Then in Scotland they say (place 1) for the same occurrence *The roof's fawed up*. Similarly on the Lancashire coalfield, in the Walkden, Little Hulton and Tyldesley areas, men will say, *You cawn't get deawn theer, it's fawn* (fallen) *up*. When I first met these expressions, I could hardly believe my ears. Such perversities really worry the helpless researcher.

Considering that mining is an old industry, there is, asterisked in the previous selection of results, a surprising number of hitherto unrecorded words. Yet most of them must have existed, at least in speech, for a long time. Consequently their absence from the *OED* and *EDD* means only that the contributors to these dictionaries never noticed them, for even all their combined efforts could not hope to trace every word, with its pronunciations and meanings, then alive in Britain. Secondly *EDD* records some words in our list and in their current meanings but only from other areas; e.g. *doggy* (deputy) for Staffordshire and Shropshire only, whereas our survey has collected it in Lancashire and Yorkshire, and *ringer* (crowbar) only for Cheshire whereas we found it in the West Riding. These could be either dictionary omissions or some proof of word movement between coalfields. On the other hand, many words listed in *EDD* were unused by our informants and rejected by them after gentle pressure or, as a last check, translation. Words of this type, which seem to have dropped or to be dropping out of existence, include *stob* and *ruin* (waste area in a mine), *colley* (coal-dust), *swad* (poor coal), and *gird* and *tack* (small prop of wood or coal). It would be interesting to know whether they have been heard anywhere recently.

Naturally miners, like all other workers, remember very clearly terms connected with their livelihood. Our oldest informant, aged seventy-nine, was said to be most absent-minded, but this never showed in his mining explanations; and certainly British mining language, despite migrations from pit to pit and from area to area, shows yet little sign of becoming one unidentifiable mass, as it has been claimed is happening to German mining language. Indeed from time to time it throws up remarkably local features. Such are the Shropshire *bonk* (self-acting incline), Leigh (Lancashire) *bonkin'* (retrieving coal from slag-heaps), and Pendleton (Lancashire) *bonk* (unwind the cage) and *bonksman* for the man who sees to that. These *o*-pronunciations, as indicated in Wright's *English Dialect Grammar* under *bank*, are typical of a north-western area including Shropshire and Lancashire. Similarly *trub* (lump of coal) and *clotch* (to disallow coal) appeared for our survey only in Yorkshire (places 3, 5), *burgy* (poor coal) only in Lancashire, *dan* (small tub) only in Shropshire and *shifter* (man who cleans out the mine ready for the next shift) only in Northumberland, coinciding with the locations given for these words in *EDD*.

Often where the layman thinks of a particular object only in outline, the industrial worker knows it in greater detail and so uses a more complicated word choice. Thus, whilst most of us think of a conventional door as a door, a window as a window, a flight of stairs as merely stairs, a carpenter thinks of *jambs, mullions, transoms, kites* and so forth. In the same way, although we usually class all underground colliery workers vaguely as *miners*, the miner gives each his rightful place in the occupational word pattern. Some of the many titles have disappeared with the twentieth-century growth of unions and the coming of nationalisation, but others are still well-known and in frequent use. The pit-head foreman may be known as the *boss, (surface-)gaffer, pit-manager* (formal term), *kayker, pit-head-man*, or by various uncomplimentary titles which all people in authority, good and bad, know it is an occupational hazard to collect. There was the *knocker-up* or *chapper-up*, who went round from house to house in the early morning rousing men for work, though nowadays when an emergency occurs this can be done by the *lorry-driver* or *odd-job-man*. There are the *banksman* controlling the shaft top and the *puller* (engine-man). The hierarchy below ground includes the *under-manager*, ranking above the *overman*, who in turn may supervise six *deputies* or *doggies* (so called, it seems, because they used to *dog* or follow their men around); and the man at the pit-bottom in charge of loading and unloading the cage is likely to be the *hanger-on, onsetter* (a more modern word), *hooker, hitcher*, or quite logically *pit-bottomer*.

Changing conditions have meant, sadly, the gradual disappearance of traditional expressions. Men in the cage at the pit-bottom and ready to be pulled up used to indicate this by shouting, e.g. 'ing on! (= Hang on!)' (3), Rap off! (4), Rap up! (5), Rap us up! (9), Knock it off! (12), Knock it up! (13). But this shouting was effective only in shallow pits, and much signalling was done by knocking with a lever or hammer and later by bells. Another case is that the *stint*, the amount of work allotted a miner, is dying in face of more modern methods and terms for them like the cycle of work, perhaps four per shift as at place 15. 'Stints is (= are) finished', said a Nottinghamshire miner (place 7), though I noticed that in spite of his comparative youth — he was thirty-two — he used in conversation the verb *stint*. Old words like *dommy* and *motty* for tub label are still well known, but only our Maltby informants remembered the *motty-hanger*, who had to fix them. As the mining environment changes, so do its words.

It is in the customs, superstitions and folklore intermingled with miners' language that much of its fascination lies. One feels that one is not just collecting words but learning more important matters impossible to convey without speech, because the word-patterns have always to be related to the society using them. For instance, there used to be a checker who would disallow whole tubs for being under weight, a management economy device later stopped by the unions. When old miners speak of this gentleman, known at Hoyland as the *clotcher*, presumably because he clutched away some of their rightful wages, all their intense hatred of him bursts out. Again, the fireman in a mine used to crawl forward on hands and knees with a long taper exploding small pockets of gas in the roof; the performer of this dangerous work, now illegal, was sometimes not a man but a boy, despite his name. Many miners did not wash their backs, in the belief that it weakened them and made them prone to accidents: and one could hardly blame my Queensbury informant for doing likewise when in his team the *on'y man 'at used to wash 'im* (the only man who used to wash himself) was killed by a pit fall. In the Rhondda, old colliers were very embarrassed at being seen naked in the pit-head baths. At Maltby, some miners carried lamps fixed to collars round their necks, but those who could not stand their heat carried them in their teeth. At Throstle Nest Colliery in the Beeston seam, men in 1920 were paid 2s. 10½d. for loading half a ton of coal and taking it 400 yards along a passage less than three feet high. This type of labour brings out unusual word-patterns at any time.

When miners from different areas meet, using different terms for the same idea, there is usually no language barrier because the idea is common to their occupation, and each miner retains his own terms. However, when they move permanently to other coalfields, confusion over technical terms can sometimes cause accidents. On the South York-shire coalfield I met an enthusiastic safety officer compiling for the Coal Board with minutest accuracy a list of local variants in an attempt to reduce accidents. He was listing differences within one small area; and when miners from many regions, bristling with their own technical terms, are transferred wholesale to another area with its own word-patterns, difficulties are bound to arise. Small wonder, then, that in 1965 the Kent branch of the National Union of Mineworkers brought out its own Glossary of Pit Terms, stating that others not in their list would 'have completely disappeared from use by February 1966', but that, should they crop up, they would be happy to explain them – to miners!

Coalminers do not live in such isolated language com-munities as remote hill-farmers or some inshore fisherman, yet they have always been rather a race apart; so that, despite movements of labour between coalfields, their language patterns seem much clearer than those of, say, the transport, catering, or construction industries. Although they do not use particular expressions because they are the 'best', the 'roughest', the 'most beautiful', or the most historically accurate for their area, their words may still fit a general pattern.

Along with farming and inshore fishing, coalmining seems to me linguistically one of our most fascinating industries. But whereas the first two continue on a fairly steady course, more and more pits are closing, and at an ever-increasing rate. At present, mining language is still vigorous and often closely attached to particular areas, and it will be some time before its terms die out altogether from the speech of the older or even younger generation. Nevertheless, the writing is on the wall, and so, in this rapidly changing world, it would well repay anyone to study coalmining language while he may still do so.

19 Steelmaking

The steel terms here discussed were gathered partly in the comfort and quiet of people's homes, and partly from visits and interviews admidst the deafening noises of giant presses, cranes and furnaces.

Although the industry, centred on Sheffield, covers a small area on the map, it embraces a vast language area with many branches, each quite specialised. The press-forge man is unlikely to know many terms well known in the foundry, and the worker in the electric-arc melting shop is in a sub-industry, with a different set of words, from the blastfurnaceman. The fact that the steel industry is comparatively modern is no drawback to the language collector, for it certainly isn't a case of racy dialect being submerged in a general, uninteresting, technical vocabulary. In such a fast-moving industry the steelworker has to think and communicate at least as quickly as the countryman. (There is, in fact, a special way of cupping your listener's ear to talk above the din of machinery.) As new processes appear, new words are needed to describe them and, where the technical terms seem too long or too learned for the man on the shop floor, he will change them or invent his own. He must talk.

All along, distinctions, expected and unexpected, abound. *Smelting* (reducing the metal from its ore) differs in meaning as well as a mere letter from *Melting*, the later process of making iron or steel. The iron bars, about four feet long, into which the ore is smelted are called, with something approaching a farmer's affection, *pigs*, and the larger ones *sows*. This latter was once the word for the large channels feeding the smaller ones — hence the name — but is now used for what are formed in the channels. Formerly there was much dodging to avoid unloading *sows* because they were so much heavier, but the operation is now done on a pig-casting machine.

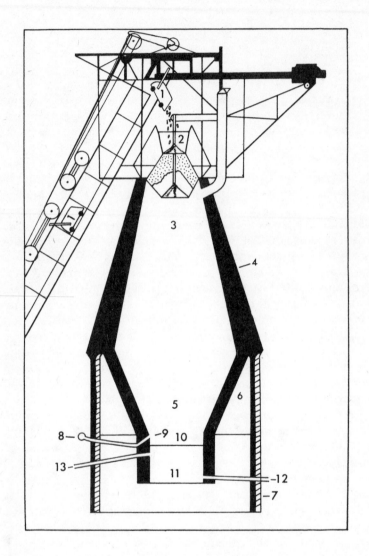

Fig. 3 Diagram of a blast-furnace

The main parts of a blast-furnace are:

1. *Skip* (small wheeled container to charge the furnace).
2. *'opper* (*hopper*, container for receiving the ore and passing it into the furnace). 3. *Throit* (throat). 4. *Stack* (chimney). 5. *Belly* (widest part of the stack). 6. *Bosh* (container round the belly). 7. *Mantle* (to support the stack). 8. *Bustle pipe* (distributing hot blast). 9. *Tweeaz* (*tuyères*, nozzles through which the air enters the furnace). 10. *(H) earth*. 11. *Bottom*. 12. *Slag-oil* or *Slag-notch* (the place where the cinders, etc., come out). 13. *Tap-oil* (small opening through which the metal is run out).*

Among so many words of Anglo-Saxon or Germanic origin it seems unusual to have *tweeaz* (*tuyères*), but even here steelworkers have twisted the pronunciation away from the French-type 'twee-airs.'† Other odd names occur like *bear*‡ for a lump of metal left in the hearth when the furnace is emptied. This is another animal name, like *pigs* and *sows* above, the metal perhaps being likened to a bear in a pit. Another curiosity, unknown to the *OED* or *EDD*, is the *go-devil,* a bucket of coke hung in the throat of the old blast-furnace to light the escaping gas. Moreover, the blast-furnaceman never pours metal but *casts* it from the furnace into the ladle, or later *teems* (pours) it from the ladle into the ingot mould. Again he has his own expressions for stopping or reducing the operation of the furnace. These include *banking* or *banking down* (adding fuel but reducing the air supply, as one does by putting *slack* on an ordinary domestic fire), *blowing down* or *steadying down* (gradually decreasing the blast), and *blowing out* (closing the furnace for repairs to the lining).

Frequent differences occur between book language and that of the shop floor. For the cupola, the type of casting furnace, although in Sheffield the pronunciation 'kyoopala' is gaining ground, 'kyoopalow' is still preferred, as it was in

*Phonetically skɪp, ɔpə¸ θɹɒɪt, stak, ¹bɛlɪ, bɔʃ, mantl, ¹bʊʊsl ¡paɪp, twɪəz, aːθ, bɔtm, ¹slag¡ɔɪl ± ¹slag¡ nɒtʃ, ¡tap¡ɔɪl.
†Phonetically twiəz.
‡Cf. *OED bear*, sb.¹, 7b.

1893.* The metal put into an open-hearth furnace, which in technical books is usually the *stock*, becomes on the shop floor the *charge*, because *stock* refers to the ingots, etc., kept in the section of the steelmill called the *stock-bay*.

Ingot defects have various names, for instance the *roke*, into which a surface blowhole rolls out; *lap*, a discontinuity on the surface where the steel 'laps' or curls over on itself; *hot clink*, where slag adheres to the ingot; *hot tear*, where the ingot comes slightly apart in being rolled; and *cold shut*, where part of the surface metal has solidified during *teeming*.

Terms used around the press forge include *porter bar* (an iron bar suspended from a crane for handling the ingot), held by a *burden chain; swage tools* (for bending and shaping the ingot); a *dye* (a 4-ft. metal container for up-ending it and impressing a deisgn upon it); *wemblies* (wide moulds introduced at the time of the Wembley Exhibition); *pickling* (dipping bars into sulphuric acid to remove scale); and *slinging* (moving ingots around by crane – to sling in the sense of hurl them, even if possible, would be sheer madness!). Also there are *dogs*, yet another animal name. According to Brandt's *Manufacture of Iron and Steel*, they are spikes in the floor for moving the ingot, but by *dogs* Yorkshire steelmen, who ought to know, mean mechanical grabs for awkwardly shaped ingots where a sling would be impossible.

A press-forging team† is led by the *codder*, and there is a corresponding verb, e.g. in *He's codding today* (of a deputy doing the work of the leader). The team includes a *stockman*, responsible for each ingot entering the *shop*, the area where the team work; an *assistant slinger*, who helps him; a *clayman*, who makes a *length lath* to determine the size of job required for the press and puts this lath on the ingot; a *press driver*, who manipulates the ingot for size; a *crane-*

---

*With current Sheffield ˈkju:pəloʊ ± ˈkju:pələ compare the statement in the *NED*, published 1893, after the definition of *cupola*, sb., 2.

† Phonetically the occupations mentioned are respectively kɔdə, stɔkmən, əˈsistənt ˈslɪnə, kleɪmən, ˈpɹɛs dɹaɪvə, ˈkɹeɪn ˌdɹaɪvə, skeɪlmən, tiːmə, tɛntə, ɹɔːlə, ʃɪəɹə, flɔːmən. *Codder* is apparently connected with *OED cod*, v¹., slang or dialectal 'to humbug, impose upon', and *teemer* is a South Yorkshire term of long standing (see *EDD, teem*, v³., 6); but *back-tonger* and *clayman* and *tenter* with the meanings above, are unrecorded in *OED* and *EDD*.

driver; and a *scaleman*, who keeps the press clear of scale. There is also the *handyman*, who keeps the shop clean: he is not called *labourer* or *sweeper-up* because then he would not qualify for a special piece-work bonus. But the gentleman in the team with the most remarkable name is the *back-tonger*, the second-in-command. He formerly stood behind the press forge with a pair of tongs to keep the ingot square, but now, his tongs having disappeared, he just signals to the crane-driver to keep it in position. Other occupational names are *teemer* (man who pours out the molten metal), *tenter* (first hand in a cupola team), and in the rolling mill the *roller* (responsible for size and section), the *shearer* (in charge of cutting), and the *floorman* (the shearer's assistant).

Electric-arc furnace work is a branch of the industry so new that it has barely had time to manufacture its own terms. So far its most noticeable features are the tendencies to shorten technical words and give them more homely names — *pressure cooker, cale-pot, kettle or chip-pan* for the electric-arc furnace, *sticks* for the electrodes, *puller-out* (fume-extractor), *lid* for both the furnace roof and a safety helmet, *dally* ('dalofrit', to mend the furnace), *connies* ('economisers', to stop heat escaping between electrode and roof), *bricks* for refractories and *dipper* for pyrometer, *blacking* (graphite dust) and *whiting* (lime). Also disconcerting is the way normal names refer to enormous objects. For example, *pens* for scrap are the size, not of sheep-pens, but of about four railway waggons; a *charging basket*, far different from, say, a shopping basket, is a metal container holding about ninety tons; and *button hooks* are the curved ends of crane arms to hold gigantic metal ladles.

In the foundry a host of tools exists, such as the *stirrer* for stirring the melt and the *skimmer* to skim off its impurities; the *chill*, a piece of cold metal put into the mould to harden it at that point; the *rapping bar* for making the mould, and *venting rods* and *vent wires* to let air into it; *sieves* and the coarser, bigger *riddles*; and *trumpets* and *tundishes*, vessels for different ways of pouring into moulds. The many types of ladle are accompanied by a variety of names, from *shanks* (hand ladles), and *two-man ladles* held and turned by two men, to enormous crane-ladles called simply *pots*. Popular etymology is keen to explain some of these words, e.g. *strickle* (the instrument to smooth the outside wall of a mould) is thought a newish word from 'strike it level,' whereas it probably goes back to the Anglo-Saxon *stricel,* an instrument for smoothing corn in a measure.*

General dictionaries note some steel words and not others, e.g. known to the *OED* are *spark arrester, tap-hole* and *sill* (the ledge in front of it), *soaking pit* (a firebrick-lined hole for cooling ingots), and *skelp* (steel strips for making into tubing); but not *wind-belt* (reservoir of air in the cupola), *tapping-pit* (next to an electric-arc furnace to draw off the metal), *stripping-stools* (for holding ingots), *slag-oil,* or even its more refined equivalent *slag-hole.*

Even when the steel is about to leave the mill, curious names are not finished with. It may be loaded on to lorries by a *wharfman* at the *wharf* or *loading dock* (loading bay), although no river or canal is in sight. Of the major British industries, farming and fishing include more old words, building language seems more straightforward, textiles has its share of curiosities, and mining expressions have a tremendous variety; but words in the steel industry are as fascinating as any.

*Cf. *EDD* and Sweet.

Part F For the Student

20 How to Collect Industrial Language

This section is intended both for students writing essays, dissertations or theses or preparing talks on industry, and for the general reader wishing to know more about how such information is collected and how to gather it himself. Space restriction naturally prevents the book being comprehensive. Ideally it should scrutinise everything, industry by industry, area after area, factory by factory, but what a mammoth and indeed impossible task that would be! However, it can help you quickly to glean relevant facts from any industry of your choice, and to classify and argue rationally from those facts, if you heed the following advice.

Choice of Industry. By taking an industry well known to you, perhaps that in which you or some of your friends or relatives work, you start with a great advantage in having suitable contacts and in being able to grasp better from the outset that industry's words and meanings. On the other hand, an industry quite new to you may attract through its sheer novelty. There are advantages either way. Of course, you need not always be limited to one industry at a time. If, say, you are holidaying in a different part of Britain, it is usually more economical and extremely interesting to sample several local industries in the same week, such as fishing, mining and farming around Whitehaven, or pottery and marine engineering at Poole.

Background Study. Before setting out, it saves much time to read fairly rapidly several books on the relevant industry, any technical dictionaries, and so on (see Bibliography). These are needed, not for remembering masses of information, some of which may be outdated, but to show or remind you what notions, processes, occupations, tools and so on are central to the industry, so that you know better what occurs in it and can thus question and decipher answers more intelligently.

Contacts. Many people, whilst not occupational language experts themselves, know who are. Lists of suitable informants may be provided by your friends, relatives, neighbours, shopkeepers, local ministers of religion, the local schoolmaster or librarian (whose trade is dealing in information of all kinds), or even by an unknown housewife cleaning her doorstep. Go along and see the possible informants recommended, for only by talking to them can you find out. A few, for one reason or another, such as suspicion towards strangers, may prove unsuitable for your purpose, but most will gladly respond and suggest more helpers.

Informants. It is no use sitting on a park seat or dropping into the nearest pub and listening or questioning at random. Ideally you should know your informant's name, address (in case follow-up questions, either face-to-face, over the phone or by post, are necessary), age, where born, birthplaces of parents, education, and how long he or she has spent in that trade or that district. (Some of these details will have been provided by your contacts, others can easily be obtained by incidental questions during your conversation.) The years up to about twenty are particularly important in forming speech habits, so beware of those who in their childhood or teens lived far away or worked in other occupations, in case they still use 'foreign' terms. You will find most people very co-operative, for it is a human characteristic to enjoy talking about one's trade and interests, even to a comparative stranger. Nearly all of us prefer talking to listening; so, provided you choose times when your helpers are not too busy, few difficulties should arise in getting them to talk.

It goes almost without saying that your helpers should be reasonably alert: something may be gained from a long rambling account, and it may give the informant himself great pleasure, but a clear answer is preferable. Those who are very hard of hearing don't make the best of informants. I vividly remember shouting into the ear-trumpet of a keen would-be helper in Northumberland, and extracting a few marvellous local answers like *hairy hubbert* for a centipede, but there must be easier ways to interview. However, it is rash to generalise: many people who are a little deaf still prove helpful and quite reliable. You can't work to dogmatic rules: see your informants, listen carefully, and act on common sense and instinct.

Number of Informants. Sometimes it is quicker and better to talk to a gang rather than to each member individually, for the members will stimulate each other. Don't rely on one person alone to represent a trade or area, since we all have so many layers of English that ours need checking with other people's — not because they are doubted, but to see what varieties exist.

Place of Interview. Not vital. I have interviewed, scribbling notes the while, on top of a cabin of a rolling ship out at sea as the compass was being adjusted, on tours of works and building sites, down the mine, in unlit village streets, in the near-darkness of cinemas, in roadside cafés and so on. A fascinating result of such interviewing is that it takes you into working men's clubs, union headquarters, canteens and so forth — places you might otherwise rarely visit. The most uncomfortable place I have used was an ant-hill in a Devonshire field, the most impressive the podium of a local council chamber. But without doubt the easiest place is in the comfort of your helper's own home, where he feels most at ease.

Initial Approach. When knocking on people's doors, it is better to be quite open about your purpose. State that you are seriously studying the occupational language and its background (as a hobby or for an educational institution). If asked, explain that you are not from the newspapers or the B.B.C. because, though some people love to be in the limelight, others would then shut up like a clam. Never relay gossip, for you would be surprised, especially in a small community, how quickly the victim hears about it and your standing drops. Assume the role of pupil, with your helper as teacher. This usually pleases him so much that he bears quite cheerfully and patiently your proofs of obvious ignorance.

Be ready for anything. You may from time to time be mistaken for an insurance salesman, baby-sitter, medical doctor or whatever. Current researchers have been mistaken for a beggar (and offered five pence by the dear lady who opened the door), a burglar coming first to spy out the land, a gun-runner, and an escaped Dartmoor convict, though fortunately such weird incidents are unlikely to happen to you. Take the rough with the smooth because, if at one time you meet an unexpected difficulty, perseverance and the law of averages will probably make the next interview go extra-smoothly.

Method of Collecting Answers. If you have unlimited time, the best is the 'squatter's' (resident investigator's) method of just listening, recording and asking no questions. Normally, however, time is important and questioning is needed. For this, easily the best is on-the-spot questioning, which conveys far more than correspondence can — more tactfully, in more detail, and much more quickly. The trouble with much older research has been that information came mostly from the study, from old glossaries, etc., and from letters. But now language researchers move around much more, their methods having been influenced by those of market research and opinion polls. Postal and book methods, along now with use of the telephone, are best regarded as useful but supplementary. What you hear from genuine first-hand informants, or take down in notes or on tape, is the crux.

Questions should wherever possible be unweighted, i.e. framed without mentioning any Standard English or other word likely to come in the answer. They may be straightforward ones like 'What do you call the widest part of a furnace?', or completing ones like 'The space between the machines is called the . . .', which the textile worker completes with *loom-gate* or whatever happens to be his own term. Only as a last resort should you attempt translation.

Mechanical Help. After answering specific questions about his industry, a speaker may be willing to talk generally about it, or his life's experiences, as the tape-recorder runs. The great point is that whatever he then says will come out quite naturally. As interviewer, you have the job of saying as little as possible, but by short questions — even by nods, smiles and looks of interest — of persuading him to keep talking. With experience, you will soon gain confidence and learn the limits of your recorder. When these machines were being developed, hundreds of clocks round England were stopped at interviewers' requests because their regular tick-tocking disturbed the rehearing of question and answer. I remember too unsuspectingly plugging a tape-recorder into a light socket in some South Hackney almshouses, whereupon because of D.C. current the machine blew up. It is to be hoped you are more mechanically minded!

Use of Pictures and Diagrams. In many cases (e.g. for flowers, birds, and details of machines), to bring these saves much time. Also, a drawing by your informant can sometimes greatly assist, or your sketch of the object in front of you as your helper tells you its parts.

Script. Approximate spelling will usually suffice for recording answers. Shorthand writers will clearly be able to use that. Better still, those conversant with phonetics and the International Phonetic Alphabet will find it invaluable for noting accurate sounds and word stress. Whatever method of notation you employ, don't record only one-word answers. Any answer is more revealing in a context, so take the whole sentence or part of it down wherever possible. Moreover, as everybody unconsciously keeps moving from one speech plane to another, and as the most genuine expressions occur in free conversation, don't forget to record incidental material — remarks about other things or to other people that are interspersed with the answers to your questions.

The rest is up to you. Now you should be well equipped for an enjoyable, wide-ranging and most useful task. Good hunting!

Appendix 1 Etymologies

For those who are historically or phonologically inclined, the chief words in various important industries have been etymologised and the findings summarised below. Where a notion in an industry is represented by many alternatives, each has been given proportionately less weight. Where different elements of a word come from different languages, this also has been duly taken into account. Originally Latin words which have entered via French have been counted statistically as French exports, but those directly from Latin, of course, as Latin. For simplicity, figures have been rounded to the nearest unit.

ETYMOLOGIES IN PERCENTAGES

	Old English	Scandi-navian	French	German	Dutch	Latin	Miscellaneous (other languages, echoic, and doubtful origins)
farming	81	2	11	—	—	2	4
mining	61	7	19	—	7	—	6
fishing	56	8	19	—	7	3	7
baking	54	11	24	—	—	—	11
textiles	43	6	17	3	3	—	28
steel	52	6	24	1	8	—	9
building	34	8	38	—	3	3	14

What stands out from the above table is how much the proportions of technical vocabulary elements differ from those in general English vocabulary. In the latter, as any word count of a passage of written or spoken English will show, the Old English element far outweighs the rest. Often it comprises 90 per cent or more of the passage, and even in the most learned writing very rarely drops below 65 per cent. This is largely due to the frequency of very common words from Anglo-Saxon like the articles *the* and *a*; pronouns and possessives like *I, it, my, hers*; conjunctions like *and, but* and *so*; and prepositions like *in, by* and *to*. Yet in the industrial vocabulary here tabulated, the Old English element is very high only in farming (81 per cent).

It is noticeable that, in general, the older the industry, the greater the Old English element, which seems historically a natural outcome. After farming, the native element is strongest in mining (61 per cent) and fishing (56 per cent), dropping low in textiles (43 per cent) and lowest of all to (34 per cent) in building construction, which of the industries sampled is the most recent. The two partial exceptions to this Old-English-for-the-oldest-industries rule are in steel, which with 52 per

cent rather surprisingly beats textiles; and inshore fishing language for
fish names, where French ones slightly outnumber Old English (42 per
cent against 38 per cent), in part probably the result of much contact
with French fisherman.

Where the Old English element is low, there is a corresponding
increase in the French and/or miscellaneous elements. Building, with 38
per cent, has easily the most French words, no doubt because the
science of architecture was developed in France; whilst textiles has an
astonishingly large miscellaneous group (28 per cent), nearly all being
words of doubtful or obscure origin.

In steel and mining, the smallish but significant Low German-cum-
Dutch element (9 per cent in steel, 7 per cent in mining) comes, it
would seem, from the science of mineralogy having been developed in
those parts of Europe. The Dutch element is often claimed to be high in
our fishing language, since they were once our bitterest rivals at sea and
have long been an important fishing nation; but at 7 per cent this Dutch
nautical element, though important, is not outstanding.

Here follows an etymological breakdown of important words
industry by industry. For precise etymologies, a dictionary like H. C.
Wyld's *Universal English Dictionary*, the *Oxford Dictionary of Etymology*, the full *Oxford English Dictionary* or a combination of such
reference works should be consulted. Common words include:

FARMING
Old English barley, barn, bridle, bullock, calf, cheese, chicken, duck,
ewe, farrow, field, foal, furrow, gate, goose, grass, halter, harvest,
headland, hen, hog, horse, lamb, mare, meadow, milk, mow, oats, pig,
plough, saddle, scythe, sheaf, sheep, shepherd, sow, stile, straw, thatch,
thresh, trough, wheat, winnow.
Scandinavian stack.
French bacon, farm, harness, reins, stable, stubble.
Latin tractor.

MINING
Old English board, brass(y), coal, collier, fall, filler, man-hole, onsetter,
overman, pit, road (passage), shaft, shift, stall, stint.
Scandinavian gate (passage).
French cage, deputy, fault, gob (waste area in mine).
Dutch pack, snap (prob. L. Du. *snappen*).

FISHING
Old English abaft, anchor, bass, beam, bearings, braid, breaker,
broadside, catch, crab, deep, east, ebb, eye (of rope), fathom, ferry,
forecastle, foresail, fish, float, flood, fluke, fresh, hatch, heave, helm,
herring, hook, knot, land, lee, lighthouse, lobster, log-book, mast,
moorings, mussel, neap, north, reach, reckoning, rope, rough, sand, sea,
seine, shank, sheer, sheet, ship, shipwright, shrimp, shroud, slack,

snood, sound, south, span, starboard, stays, stem, stock, swell, tide, twine, warp, wash, watch, water, wave, weigh, west, windward, winkle, witch, yard.
Scandinavian bait, bank, harbour, low, muggy, rawky, scar, scud, skate, squally, -swain (in boatswain, coxswain).
French bail, barb (on hook), broach, cabin, calm, cockle, crayfish, current, gaff, haul, jib, launch, line, mackerel, quarter, quay, ray, salmon, scallop, spawn, sturgeon, stranu, suck, trawler, turbot.
Latin pier, truck (on mast), winch.
Dutch becket, boom, bow, bulwark (prob. Du. *bolverk*), gybe, kit, marline, skipper, splice, whiting.

BAKING
Old English barm, bread-pot, crumb, docker (for piercing cobs, etc.), dough, green (underripe), knead, loaf, riddle, sad (heavy), sieve, spring (amount a loaf rises), yeast.
Scandinavian scuffle (mop).
French cake, crown (of oven), crust, flour, foxy (reddish-brown, of yeast), gluten, sole (of oven).

TEXTILES
Old English doffer, fettler, lap, loom, reacher, shuttle, spindle, tease, warp, weft, yarn.
French bobbin, mule (type of spinning machine), piecing, skein, tentering (finishing process).

STEEL
Old English chill, crane-driver, dye, fettle, floorman, handyman, hearth, hopper, iron, ladle, melt, riddle, shank, shearer, sill, steel, stirrer, stock, strickle, teem, wharfman.
Scandinavian cast, mould, skip (container to charge furnace), stack (of furnace).
French billet, charge (a furnace), forge, foundry, porter bar, roller, skimmer, tenter, trumpet (the tool), tuyère, vent.
Dutch pickle (dip in acid), rabble (for stirring furnace), sling, smelt.

BUILDING
Old English drain, draw-pin, eaves, frog (hollow in brick), hip (on roof), house, king-post, lath, queen-post, rafter, ridge, riser, stile (door rail), strut, tie-beam, tread, waney (bevelled), weatherboard, winder.
Scandinavian lag (pipes), skirting.
French architrave, batten, breeze block, carcass (lay pipes in a house), course (of bricks), cavity, corbel, escutcheon, gutter, hod, jamb, joist, lintel, mullion, newel, plumb, quoin, render, sewer, stuff (timber), transom, truss, valley (on roof), verge.
Latin fixer (who installs cupboards, etc.).
Dutch shore, spout.

Appendix 2 Miscellaneous Industries

Here are some traditional terms from several fascinating industries which there has been little space to mention. No doubt you will enjoy adding to the list:

BREWING
ale a liquor brewed from malt and generally stronger than beer. Traditionally, however, in Cumberland and Somerset, a weak beer.
crap sediment of beer or ale at bottom of barrel.
ciderkin the washings after the best cider has been made.
glox of liquids, to gurgle when rolled about inside a barrel.
malt-worm a tippler.
nappy frothy.
nitty sparkling.
roil of beer, to become thick.

CANALS
angle of tumblehome angle of incline inwards from the deck's widest point, at which a barge's upper structure will pass under a bridge (cf. *OED*, *tumble*, sb., 11).
the animal Older boatmen who had no money to buy a horse always referred thus, and not jokingly, to their donkey or mule.
Burnidgeham Birmingham — not a canalman's slip of the tongue, but caused because some of them could not read.
cut always for canal.
gas-boat Stoke area word for a coal-tar boat because it went to the gas-works.
go on land to retire, live in a house as distinct from on a boat. The real contrast, however, is smaller, because the house may be at the canal side and the boats never put out to sea.
inside towards the tow-path side; and *outside*, towards the canal's far side. If the boat approaches the other bank, *inside* becomes *outside* and vice versa.
Josher boat made by Fellowes, Moreton & Clayton (from Joshua, Christian name of one of the directors).
straps always for ropes.

FOOTWEAR
barmskin cobbler's leather apron.
cap(el)/spetch leather patch on toe of shoe or clog.

lingan/lingle shoemaker's thread.
naiglet/taglet/tib/tip/tug/stud/tab/nib metal tag on end of lace.
seat final course of leather in a boot heel.
slotch of too-large shoes, to slip about.
snob/souter/cordwainer cobbler.
stirrup shoemaker's strap to keep the last firm upon his knee.
shovon/shoe-string/shoe-tie/twang/thong/whang shoelace.

GLASS-MAKING
cratch glazier's case for carrying glass and tools.
fret/grog broken glass.
kinney corner of a furnace.
punty iron tube used for glass-blowing.

HATTING
breward/flipe/rim hat-rim.
crow a low-crowned hat; rejected work.
curl edge of hat brim which turns over.
neb peak of a cap.
pad a delivery of work.
private a workman's own trademark.

HOP-GROWING
liver-hops the hops at the bottoms of the poles which get too little sun
to ripen them.
long-bob a small fly which infects hops.
lucky-hop a hop in which leaves grow in the berry.
oast kiln for drying hops (from Old English *āst*).

LEAD-MINING
coe small hut over climbing shaft of lead mine, where miners keep their
tools or change their clothes.
groove lead mine
polin(g) stake or plank to support the roof.
wogh a rock on the side of a vein.

POTTERY
blunger pole used for stirring; large tub with revolving arms into which
the liquid clay is poured.
burn a quantity of ware sufficient for one person to carry.
dod iron plate with one or more holes through it.
pot-bank pottery.
shrager coarse pot of marl for baking wares.

QUARRYING
cratch quarryman's stool with sloping top and two sides.
quarr(el) quarry.
slot a wedge-shaped block of stone *in situ*.

SALT-MINING

benching getting bed of rock salt down to the 'sole' of the mine after the roofing drift has been made.

cats masses of salt formed under a pan when it leaks.

draught quantity of salt taken out each time the pan is cleared.

fresh rain that falls on top of the brine in a brine-cistern, and floats on top.

kill to weigh salt.

leach the fully saturated lime which drains from the salt or is left in the pan when the salt is drawn out.

lead a salt-pan.

lump-rock large piece of rock salt obtained in working.

lump-salt salt obtained by boiling the brine.

pike one-pronged instrument for lifting and handling lumps of salt.

STONEMASONRY

banker bench or rough table on which a mason rests the stone he is working.

boast to dress stone with a mason's broad chisel.

gallet/garret insert small pieces of stones in the joints of stone or rough masonry.

mash large hammer for breaking stones.

scolch to gouge.

TIN-MINING

pillion tin which remains in the slag after the first melting.

row coarse, undressed tin ore; refuse from the stamping mills.

stream to wash the surface deposits of tin.

tin-dresser man who prepares tin ore for the smelting furnace.

tribute percentage of share of produce of a mine claimed by a miner. Hence *tributer* for a man working on this system.

Select Bibliography

A GENERAL REFERENCE WORKS

Brook, G. L., *English Dialects* (Deutsch, 1963).
——, *Varieties of English* (Macmillan, 1973).
Evans, H. *Editing and Design*, bk I *Newsman's English* (Heinemann, 1972).
Foster, Brian, *The Changing English Language* (Macmillan, 1960; Penguin, 1970).
Franklyn, J., *Dictionary of Rhyming Slang* (Routledge, 1960).
Gowers, E., *The Complete Plain Words* (2nd. ed., revised by Sir Bruce Frazer: Penguin, 1973).
Hogben, L., *The Vocabulary of Science* (Heinemann, 1969).
Jackson, I., *The Provincial Press and the Community* (Manchester University Press, 1971).
Jones, D., *An English Pronouncing Dictionary* (11th ed., London, 1950).
The Oxford English Dictionary (OED), with *Supplements*: vol. I, A–G (1972); vol. II, H–P; vol. III, Q–Z and Bibliography (both forthcoming).
Partridge E., *Dictionary of Slang and Unconventional English*, 3rd ed., London, 1949.
The Penguin English Dictionary (1958).
Savory, T. H., *The Language of Science* (Deutsch, 1953).
Transactions of the Yorkshire Dialect Society (TYDS).
Wakelin, M. F., *English Dialects: an Introduction* (Athlone Press, 1972), especially Chapter 8 on occupational dialects.
Wright, J., *The English Dialect Dictionary* (Oxford, 1898–1905) *(EDD)*.
Wyld, H. C., *The Universal Dictionary of the English Language*, 2nd ed., London, 1952.

B PARTICULAR INDUSTRIES

Aviation
Barry, W. S., *The Language of Aviation* (Chatto & Windus, 1962).

Brewing
Ambler, P. J., 'The Terminology of the Beer Barrel at Queensbury in the West Riding', *TYDS* (1954) pp. 21–6.

Coalmining
Heaton, S., 'The Occupational Language of a Blackhall Coal-Miner, *Journal of the Lancashire Dialect Society* (1972), pp. 19–21.

Llewellyn, E. C., *The Influence of Low Dutch on the English Vocabulary* (Oxford, 1936) Chapter 11.

Wright, P., 'Coal-Mining Language: a Recent Investigation', *Patterns in the Folk Speech of the British Isles*, ed. Wakelin, M. F. (Athlone Press, 1972).

Farming

Cowley, W., 'The Technique and Terminology of Stacking and Thatching in Cleveland', *TYDS* (1954) pp. 35—40.

Goundrill, G. J., 'Ploughing and Pressing Wheat on the Wolds Thirty Years Ago', ibid., pp. 40—7.

Hudleston, N. A., 'Farm Waggons of N.E. Yorkshire', *TYDS* (1952).

———— 'Notes of Yorkshire words relating to Horses', *TYDS* (1959).

Orton, H., et al., *Survey of English Dialects* (Leeds, 1962—71) Part 1 of each volume.

Fishing

Binns, A. L., 'Humber Words', *TYDS* (1957) pp. 10—25.

Nance, R. M., *Glossary of Cornish Sea-Words*, ed. Pool, P.A.S. (Marazion, 1963).

Tindall, M. S., 'Crabs and Lobster Fishing at Staithes in the North Riding', *TYDS* (1950) pp. 44—50.

Wright, P., 'Proposal for a Short Questionnaire for use in Fishing Communities', *TYDS* (1964) pp. 27—32.

———— 'Fishing Language around England and Wales' [with on-the-spot results from fifty one widely scattered places] *Journal of the Lancashire Dialect Society* (1968).

Nail-making and Clogging

Moody, F. W., 'The Nail and Clog-Iron Industries of Silsden in the West Riding', *TYDS* (1951) pp. 39—48.

Quarrying

Sykes, D. R., 'Dialect in the Quarries at Crosland Hill, near Huddersfield, in the West Riding', *TYDS* (1954) pp. 26—31.

Textiles

Moody, F. W., 'Some Textile Terms from Addingham in the West Riding', *TYDS* (1950) pp. 37—43.

Index

abbreviations, 102-8
abstract nouns, 58
advertising, 30, 117-23
Air Force jargon, 5
—————slang, 5, 25
air transport terms, 29
alliteration, 48, 122
alternatives, 139-41
ambiguity, 50, 55
Americanisms, 15, 30-1
Anglo-Saxon, 11-12, 195-7
animal names, 62-4
Arabic, 14
architectural terms, 13
asking the time, 78
auctions, 70, 125
avoided words, 138-9

back formations, 15
back slang, 86
bacteriology slang, 62
bakers, 22-3
baking terms, 64, 195, 197
barrow-boys, 23
basketball signs, 71
belonging, appeal to sense of, 119
bingo language, 89
biological terms, 110
—————abbreviations, 106-7
—————slang, 84
bluntness of language, 57-60
botanical names, 13, 110
bowling terms, 65, 71
brewing terms, 198
building terms, 62, 108, 195-7
bus terms, 21

canal terms, 48, 199
car auctions, 125
—————terms, 16, 29, 77
carpenter's conversation, 149-50
Celtic loans, 11-12
changes of meaning, 41-5
chemical engineering terms, 42
chemistry department, 62

circumlocution, 136
City words, 29
clergyman's voice, 49
clerical terms, 63
clichés, 134
clog terms, 19-21
clothing terms, 29, 165
clumsy, words for, 59
coalmining terms, 32, 45-6, 61-2, 70,
    138-9, 169-80, 195-6
collecting language, ways of, 189-93
colloquialisms, 5-6
commercial jargon, 136-7
committee language, 154-5
comparisons, 63, 108-10, 128-9
compounds, 16
computer terms, 25, 62, 142
conciliators' language, 156
context, 42-3, 46, 105
conversations, 85, 147-51
cricket terms, 5
—————signs, 71
crossing industries, terms, 24-5

deaf-and-dumb language, 70
degradation, 41
dentists' language, 2
dialect, local, 3-4, 6,26-7
—————social, 3-4
directions, 143-4
dirty, words for, 59
distillation terms, 61
domestic terms, 29
doubtful etymologies, 16
dressmaking terms, 13, 161
drug-taking slang, 86
drunk, words for, 59
Dutch loans, 11, 14, 195-7

echoic words, 11, 15-16
education, 154-6
electrical engineering terms, 4, 69, 111
—————abbreviations, 103, 105-6
—————slang, 84
electronics terms, 29-30, 65

elevation, 41
engine noises, 16
equations, 107, 152
etymologies, 11-18, 195-7
euphemisms, 76-7, 115-6, 130-4
exaggerations, 128
exhausted, words for, 60
extension, 42
extra syllables, 47

fairs, 78
family titles, 101
famous people's names, 66
farming words, 1, 11-12, 57, 195-6
farm labourers' conversations, 150-1
fashion words, 29
fear, appeals to, 119
feasts, 78
feminine terms, 17, 90
financial language, 137-8
fish-hawkers, 23
fishing terms, 1, 11-12, 17-18, 33, 35,
    42, 64-5, 195-7
────── comparisons, 109
────── conversation, 147-9
folk etymology, 11, 15, 44
folklore, 144-5
food, words for, 13, 59, 80,
    166-8
footwear terms, 198
foolish, words for, 58
'foreign' words, 34-8
French loans, 11, 13-14, 195-7
friendliness of language, 57-60
front slang, 86-7
furniture, 164

gardening terms, 13, 110
gearbox noises, 16
gender, 51-2
geography, 143-4
geological terms, 45-6
German loans, 11, 14, 195-7
glass-making terms, 198
golf language, 62
gossip, words for, 60
grammar, 47, 50-4
graphic shortenings, 102
Greek loans, 11, 13, 26, 110, 195-7
grimness of language, 128-9
gypsies, 23-4

hairdressing terms, 13, 109
────── slang, 85
────── abbreviations, 104
hatting terms, 198
hit, words for, 60
holidays, 78-81
homosexual, words for, 95
hop-growing terms, 199
household words, 29, 161-8
houses, types of, 162

illnesses, occupational, 141
Indian terms, 14
industrial action terms, 29, 78
initials instead of words, 104-8
informal language, 5-6
intelligibility, 127, 145-6, 152-3
intensifiers, 53-4
internationalisation, 41
intonation, 37-8
Italian loans, 11, 14

jargon, 4-5
journalese, 113-7

knocker-up, 22

Latin loans, 11, 13, 110, 195-7
layers of language, 3-6
lead-mining terms, 199
left-handed, words for, 59
legal jargon, 5, 137
loan words, 11-18, 195-7
local dialect, 3-6, 26-7, 50-1
lorry-drivers' sign language, 70-1
lost syllables, 47, 102-3
love, words associated with, 168
lying, 129-30

malapropisms, 44-5
McLuhan, Marshall, 152-3
Manx, 12
mass media, 112-26
mathematical language, 107
mechanical engineering terms, 102
medical language, 13, 27, 36, 59, 111,
    141
Merchant Navy slang, 85
metaphors, 108-110
midden-man, 21-2
military commands, 49
milkmen, 23
mineralogical terms, 14

mining, *see* coalmining, lead-mining
   and tin-mining
misers, words for, 60
mispronunciations, 43-5

narrowing, 41-2
nautical terms, 1, 11-12, 17-18, 33, 35,
   42, 64-5, 195-7
naval slang, 85
navvies' slang, 85
new sciences, 28-9
new words, 26-33
newspaper language, 113-7
nonsense elaborations, 135
——— words for, 59
notices, unusual, 123-6
nursing abbreviations, 104-5
——— slang, 85

obituary language, 114
obscure etymologies, 16
Old English, 11-12, 195-7
Old Norse, 11-13, 195-7
old trades, 19-24
onomatopoeic words, 11, 15-16
overseas doctors, English of, 36

parallel etymologies, 17
pawnbrokers, 22
peat-cutting, 27
pedlars, 24
personification, 64-6
physical states, words for, 59
physics, language of, 107
pidgin English, 101
postmen, 59
pottery terms, 199
prefixes, 16-17
prepositions, 11
pride, appeals to, 118
printing, sign language, 69
prison slang, 86
pronouns, 52-3
pronunciation, 47-8
puns, 122

quarrying terms, 199

racecourse language, 71
radio language, 112
rag-and-bone man, 21
railway terms, 19, 24-5, 62, 65
redundancy terms, 76

reduplication, 15
repaired, words for, 59
repetition, 135
research methods, 189-93
rhyme, 48, 122
rhyming slang, 87-9
rock names, 45-6
rooms, 162-3
rubbish, words for, 139
rugby signs, 71
Russian, 14-15

salmon types, words for, 46
salt-mining terms, 200
sayings, proverbial, 144
Scandinavian loans, 11-13, 195-7
sciences, words for new, 28-9
scything, 27
sergeant-major's voice, 49
semantics, 41-6
semaphore, 70
sensationalism, 113-5
sex, appeals to, 118-9
——— change of, 51-2
sexual language, 93-7
sheep-scoring numerals, 12
shift-names, 141-2
ship-repairing, 69
sign language, 67-72
simplification, 101-11
slang, 4-5, 26, 82-9
soccer terms, 112
——— signs, 71
social dialects, 3-4
sounds, 47-50
space-fillers, 135
Spanish loans, 11, 14
speed of talk, 127
spelling, 142-3
spoonerisms, 44
stage-coach terms, 24
station-announcer's voice, 49-50
status symbols, 164-5
steel industry terms, 25, 61, 64, 181-6,
   195-7
——— sign language, 68-9
Stock Exchange terms, 46, 62
stonemasonry terms, 200
street-names, 33
stress, 37-8, 48-9
student-teacher's throat, 49
style, 55-6
suffixes, 17

superstition, 144-5
surf-riding terms, 62, 85-6
surnames, occupation, 18-19
swearing, 90-3
symbols, 107, 152
synonyms, 17

tangled, words for, 59
tautology, 134
technicality of words lost, 42
television language, 112-13, 122
ten-pin bowling terms, 62, 85
terseness of language, 128-9
textile terms, 14, 195-7
——— comparisons, 109-10, 146
——— sign language, 69-70
thatching, 27
threshing, 27
tic-tac man, 71
tin-mining terms, 200
titles, occupational, 140-1
toilet, words for, 97-8, 133
tool names, 66, 139-40
trade terms, 29
transport slang, 85
traps in language, 41-6

unchanged plurals, 52
uncouth language, 90-8
understatements, 128
unrecorded words, 31-2
untidy, words for, 163
U.S.A. loans, 15, 30-1

variants, 139-41
verbal forms, 54-5
violent words, 60
vivid compounds, 16
voicing, unusual, 49-50
vowel pronunciations, 47-8

wages, words for, 75
wakes, 78-9
war terms, 14, 26
washing terms, 165-6
weak, words for, 59
weather sayings, 144
Welsh terms fighting English, 35
white lies, 129-30
wives' language, 155-6
women's magazines, 161-2
work, words for, 77-8
work-mates, words for, 75